MIDDLESBROUGH COUNCIL

Songs in Sign for Children

Songs selected and
signed by
Elaine McBean

illustrated by
David Hodgson

Beverley School
Middlesbrough.

Introduction

We have been singing and signing at Beverley School for several years now. From a small beginning, a class item on a Christmas concert, the activity has gradually gained momentum so that it is now a vital part of the curriculum.

Its functions are many: improved language skills, memory, speech, signing, creative expression. However, the best recommendation for its practice that we can offer is that it's fun.

This book contains a few of the songs we enjoy. We hope that you will have as much pleasure from them as we do.

Guide to drawings

Each drawing represents a signed word or phrase.
Words in italics are not signed.
Hands drawn in dotted lines show the **start** of the sign.
Hands drawn in solid lines show the **finish.**

Contents

Sing a Rainbow

Red and yellow
And pink and green
Purple and orange and blue
I can sing a rainbow
Sing a rainbow
Sing a rainbow too
Listen with your eyes
Listen with your eyes
And sing everything you see
You can sing a rainbow
Sing a rainbow
Sing along with me
Red and yellow
And pink and green
Purple and orange and blue
Now we can sing a rainbow
Sing a rainbow
Sing a rainbow too

Red

and

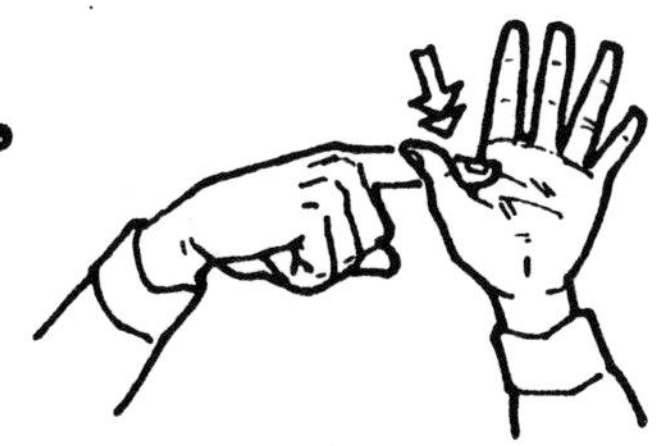

yellow

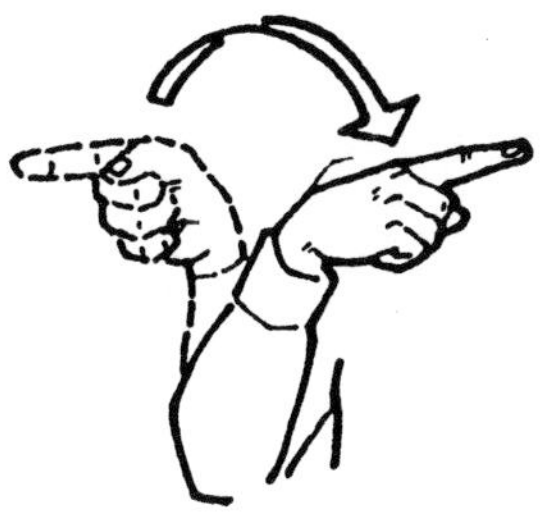

And

pink

and

green

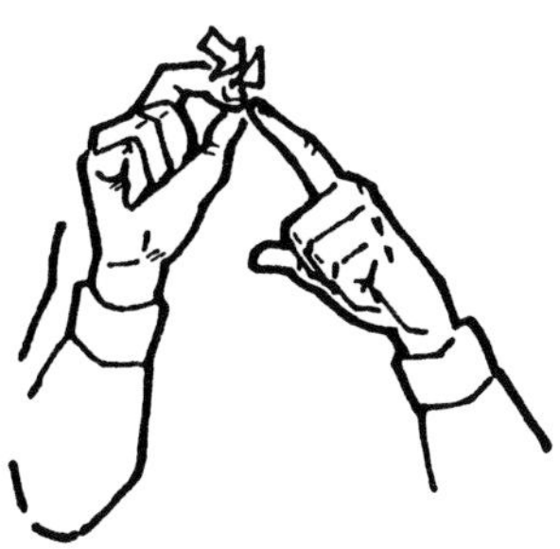

Purple

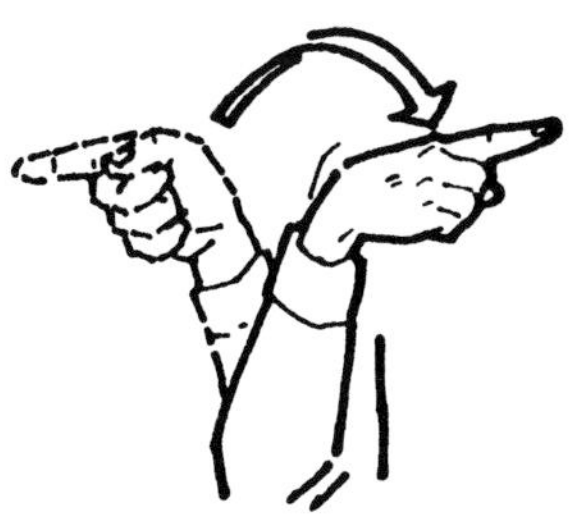

and

orange

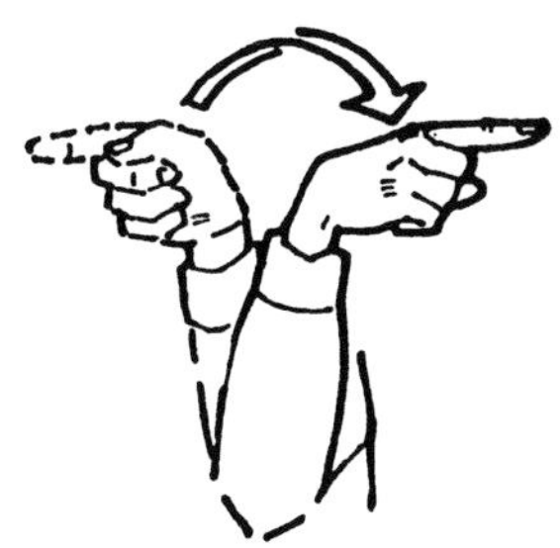

and

blue

I can sing a rainbow

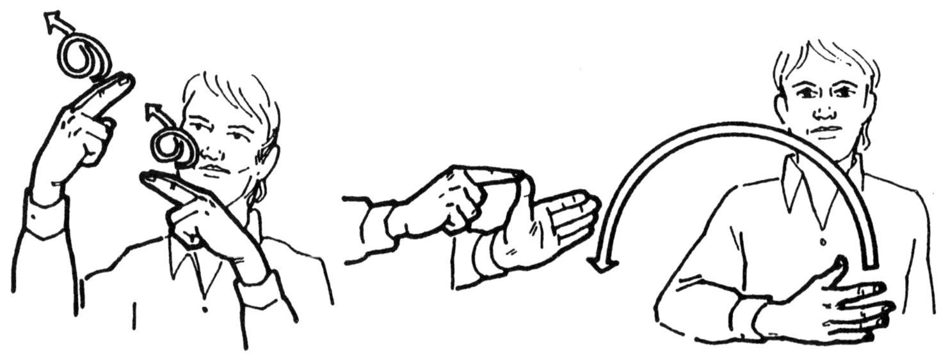

Sing a rainbow

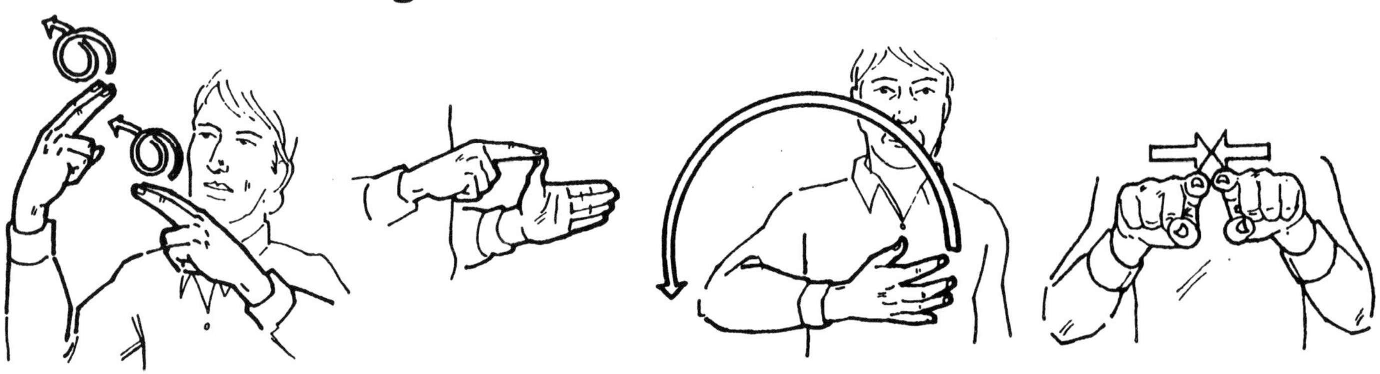

Sing a rainbow too

Listen

with

your

eyes

Listen

with

your

eyes

And

sing

everything

you

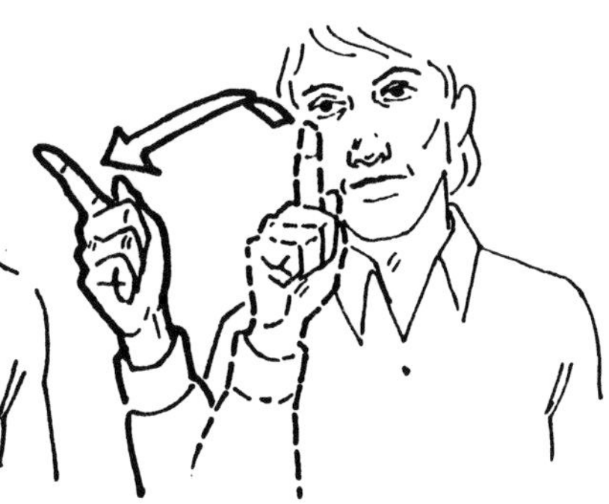
see

You can sing a rainbow

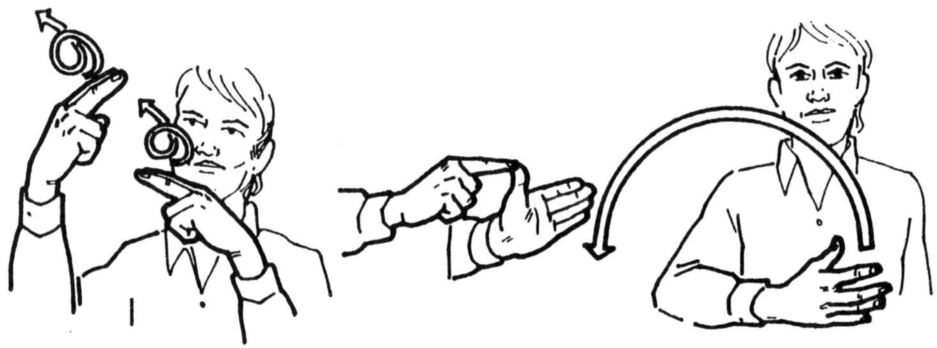

Sing a rainbow

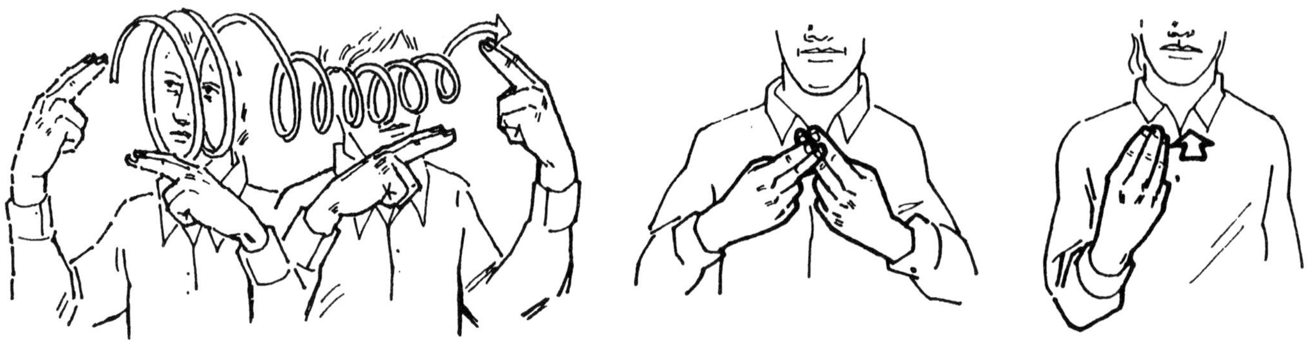

Sing along with me

Red

and

yellow

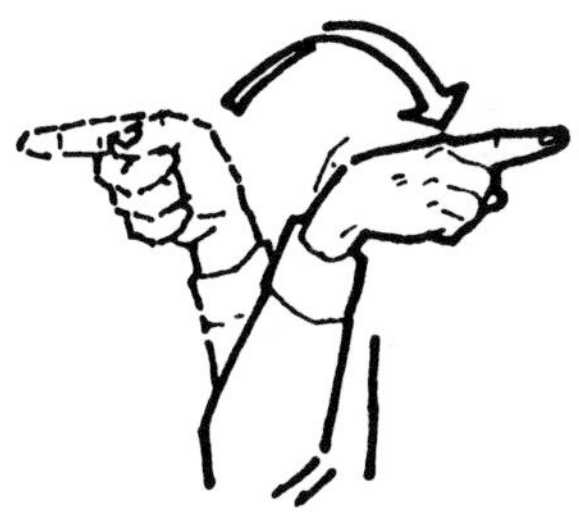
And

pink

and

green

Purple

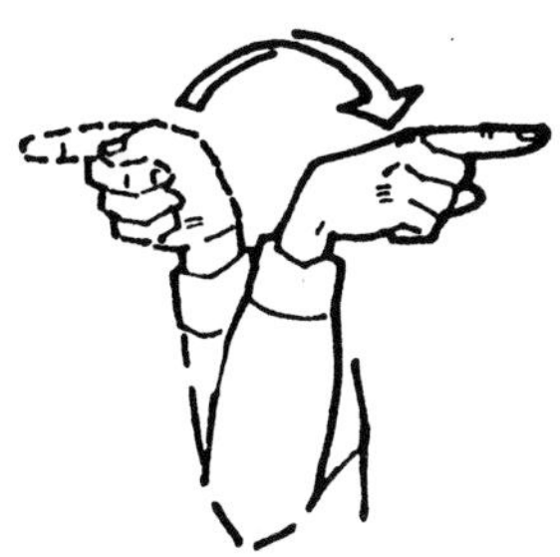
and

orange

and

blue

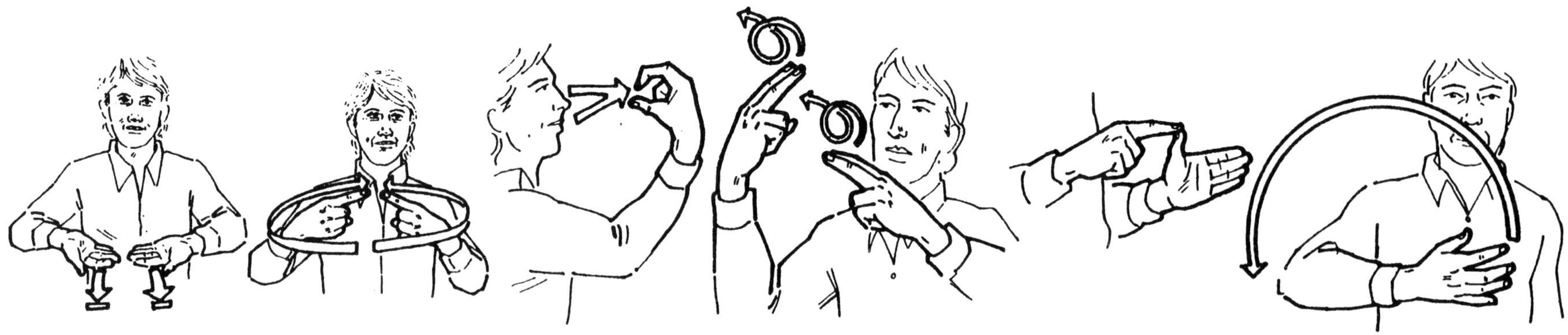

Now we can sing a rainbow

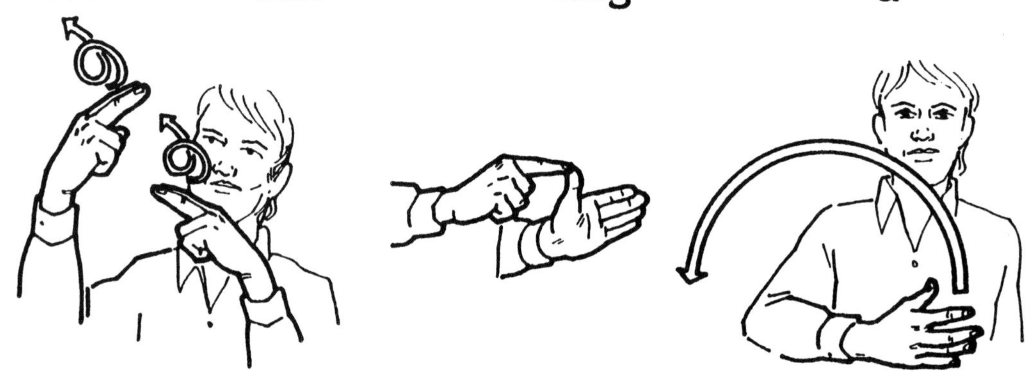

Sing a rainbow

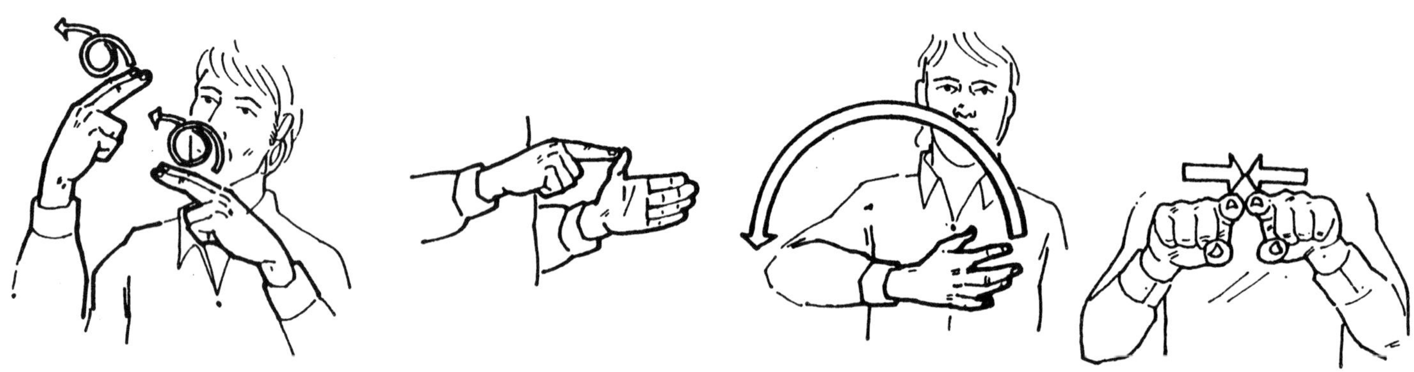

Sing a rainbow too

Happy Birthday

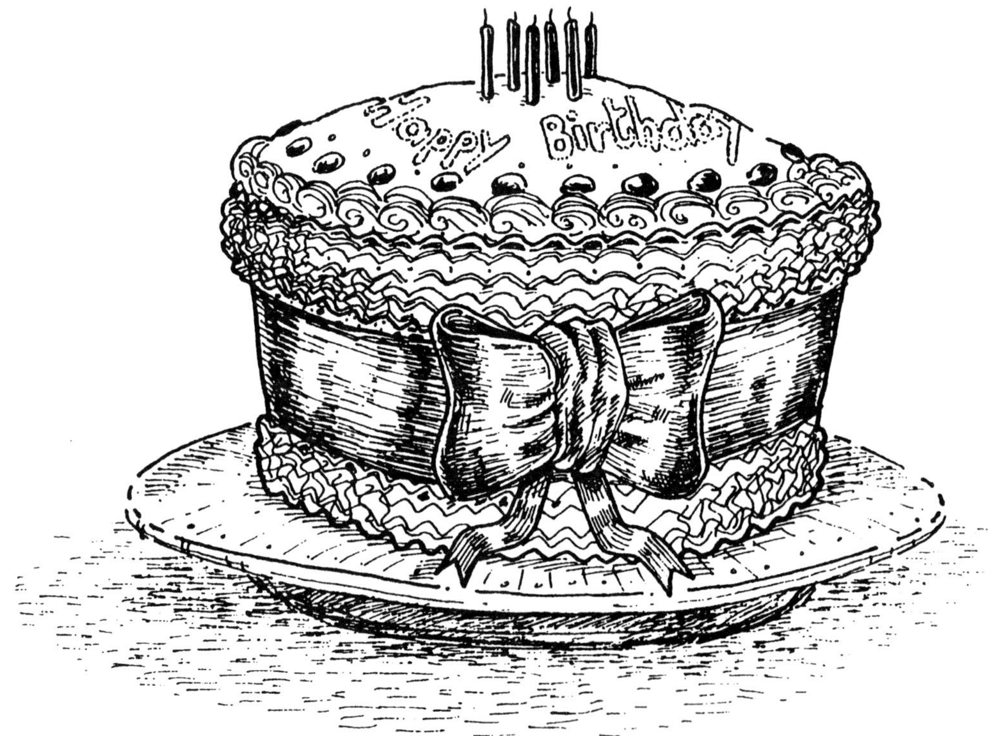

Happy Birthday to you
Happy Birthday to you
Happy Birthday dear " .... "
Happy Birthday to you.

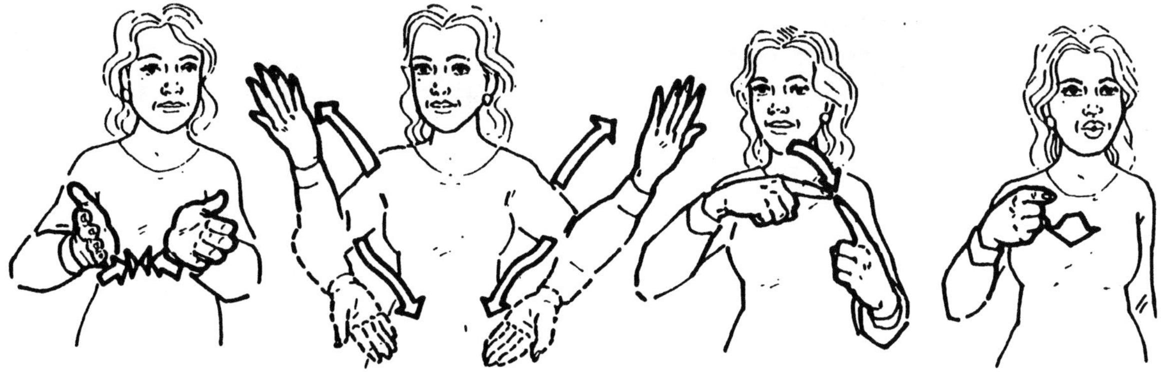

Happy Birthday to you
Happy Birthday to you

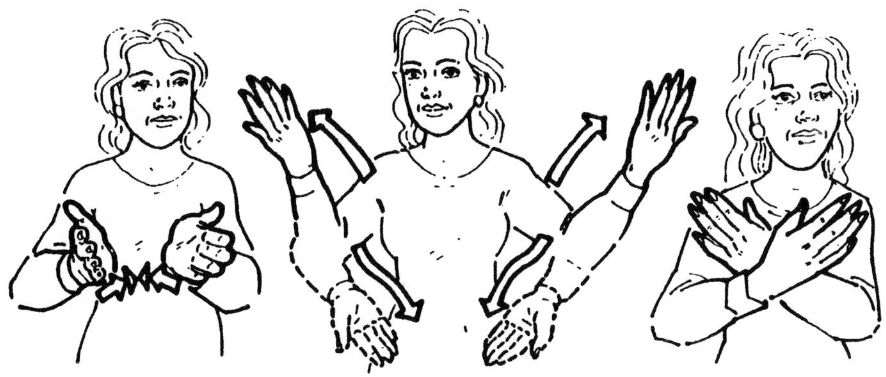

Happy Birthday dear " .... "

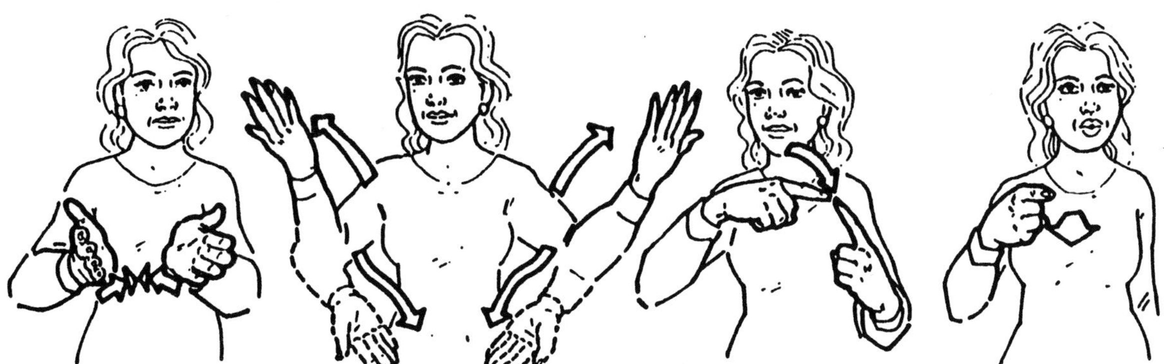

Happy Birthday to you.

Praise Him, Praise Him

1. Praise Him, Praise Him
All you little children
God is love, God is love.

2. Love Him, Love Him
All you little children
God is love, God is love.

3. Thank Him, Thank Him
All you little children
God is love, God is love.

(1) Praise Him, Praise Him

All you little children

God is love, God is love.

(2) Love Him, Love Him

All you little children

God is love, God is love.

(3) Thank Him,

Thank Him

All

you

little

children

God

is

love,

God

is

love.

Pussy Cat, Pussy Cat

1. Pussy Cat, Pussy Cat
Where have you been?
I've been to London
To see the new queen.

2. Pussy Cat, Pussy Cat
What did you there?
I frightened a little mouse
Under her chair.

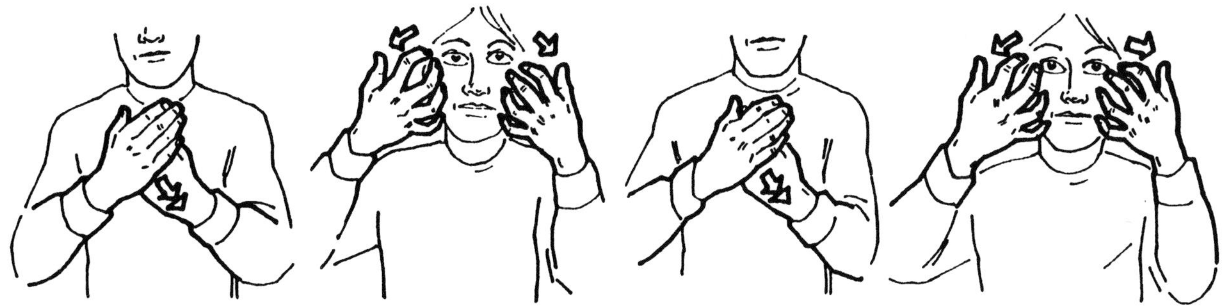

(1) Pussy Cat, Pussy Cat

Where have you been?

I've been to London

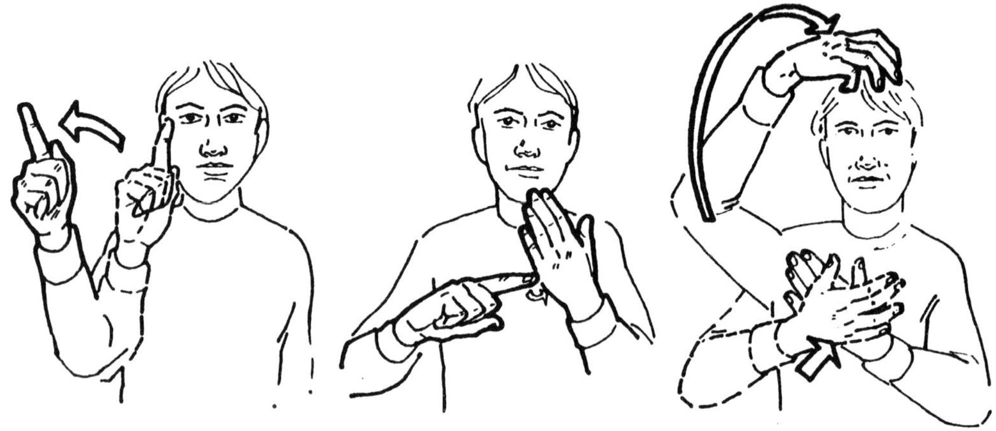

To see the new queen.

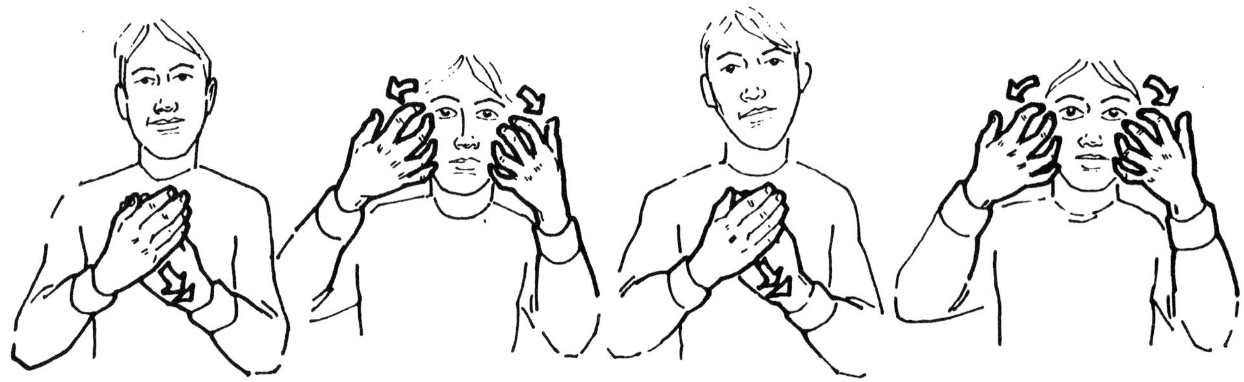

(2) Pussy Cat, Pussy Cat

What did you there?

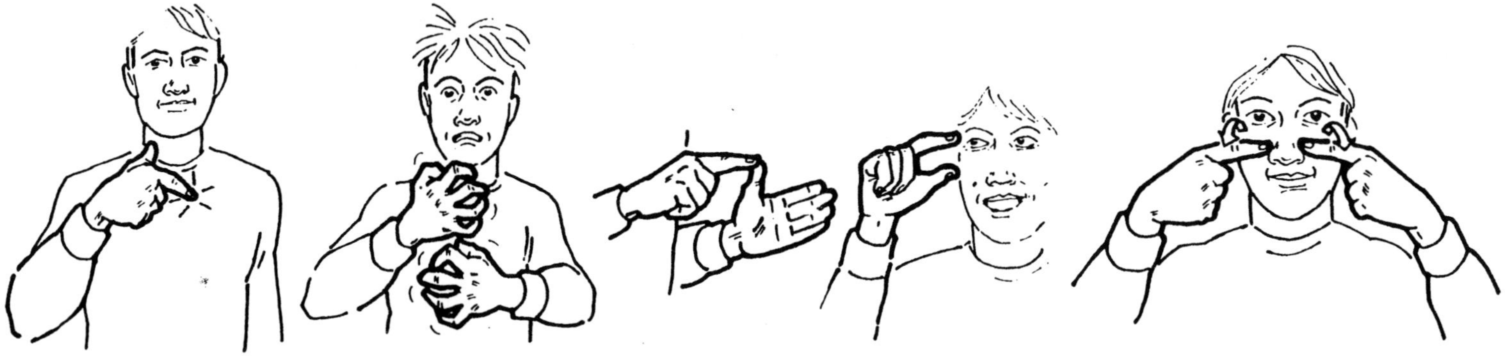

I frightened a little mouse

Under her chair.

Hickory Dickory Dock

Hickory-Dickory-Dock
The mouse ran up the clock
The clock struck one
The mouse ran down
Hickory-Dickory-Dock.
Tick-tock, tick-tock.

Hickory- Dickory- Dock

The mouse ran up the clock

The clock struck one

The

mouse

ran

down

Hickory-

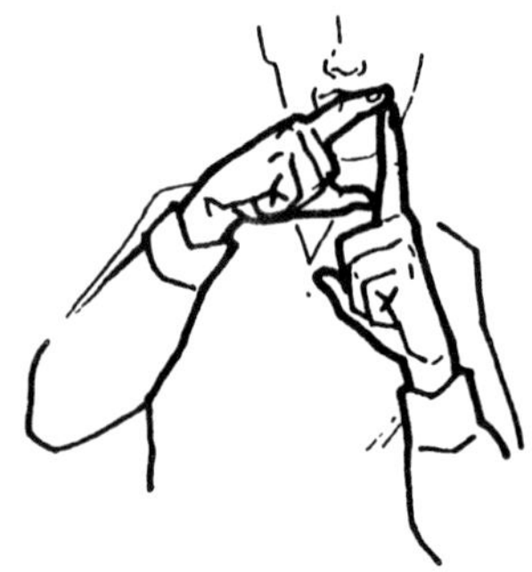

Dickory-

Dock.

Tick-tock,

tick-tock.

Hush My Baby

1. Hush my baby
   Hush my little baby
   Mother rocks you on her knee
   Sings to you so quietly
   Hush my baby
   Hush my baby.

2. Sleep my baby
   Sleep my little baby
   Mother watches carefully
   While you sleep so peacefully
   Sleep my baby
   Sleep my baby.

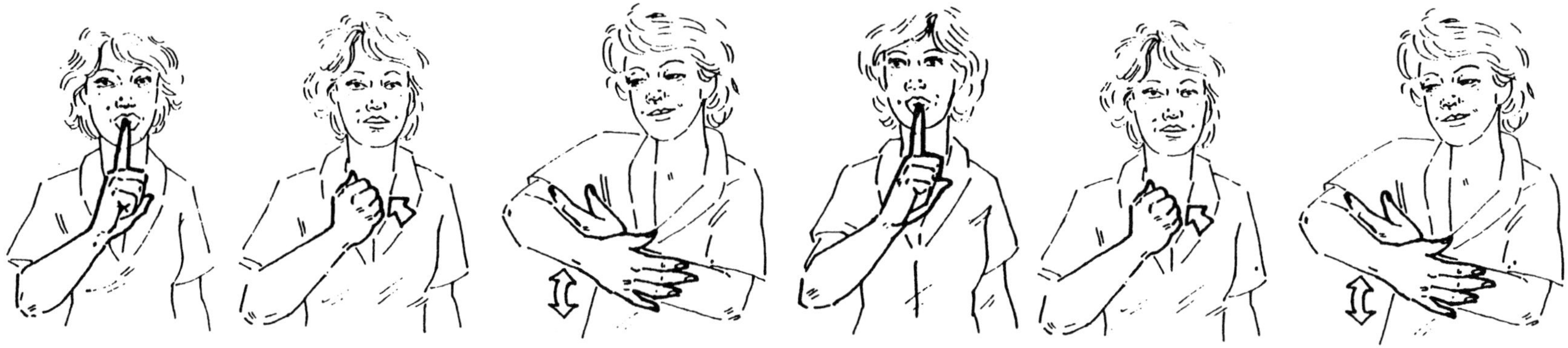

(1) Hush my baby Hush my *little* baby

Mother rocks *you on her knee* Sings *to you* so quietly

Hush my baby Hush my baby.

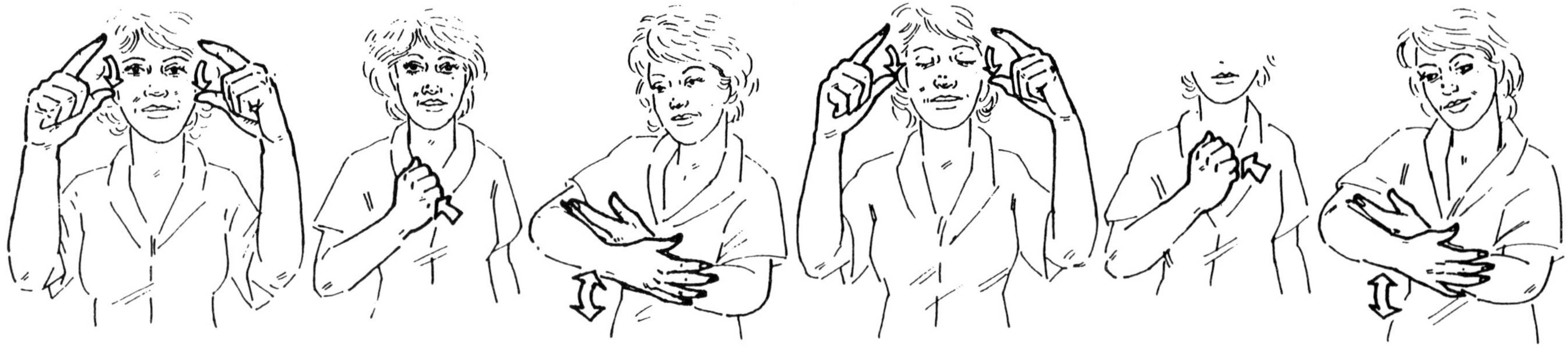

(2) Sleep my baby Sleep my *little* baby

Mother watches carefully

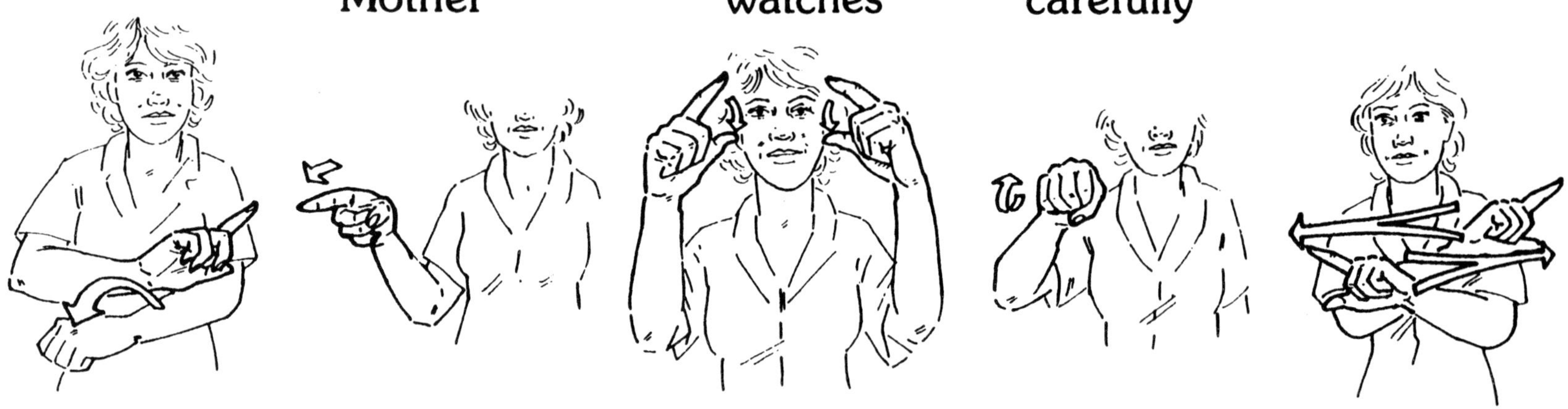

While you sleep so peacefully

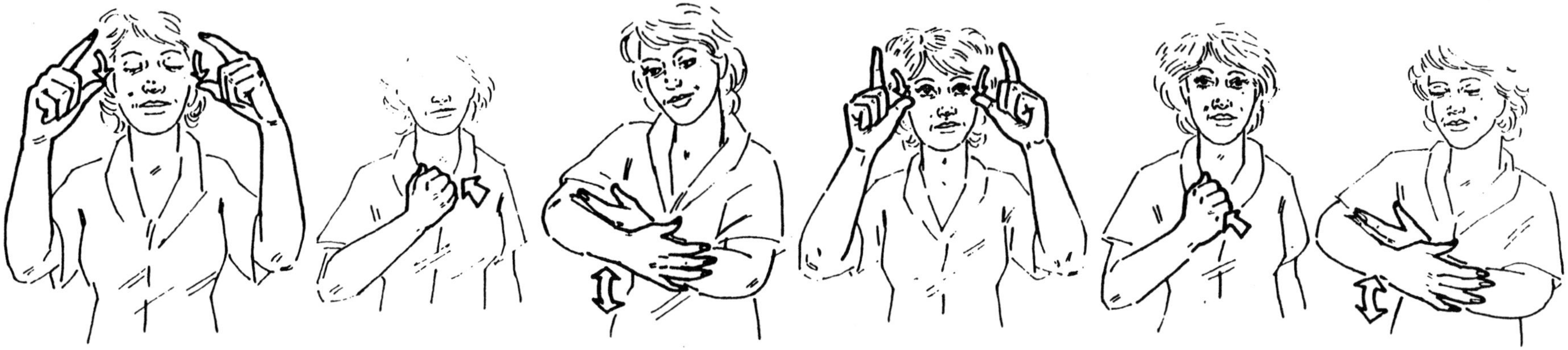

Sleep my baby Sleep my baby.

Ten in the Bed

1. There were ten in the bed
   And the little one said
   "Roll over! Roll over!"
   So they all rolled over
   And one fell out

2. There were nine in the bed
   And the little one said
   "Roll over! Roll over!"
   So they all rolled over
   And one fell out

3. There were eight in the bed ...

4. There were seven in the bed ...

5. There were six in the bed ...

6. There were five in the bed ...

7. There were four in the bed ...

8. There were three in the bed ...

9. There were two in the bed ...

10. There was one in the bed ...

11. There were none in the bed
    And the little one said
    "Good night! Good night!"

(1) There were ten in the bed

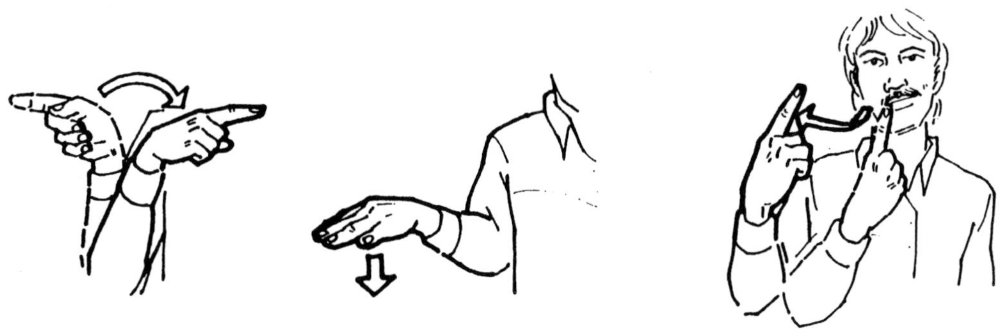

And *the* little one said

"Roll over! Roll over!"

So they all rolled over

And one fell out

(2) There were nine in the bed

And *the* little one said

"Roll over! Roll over!"

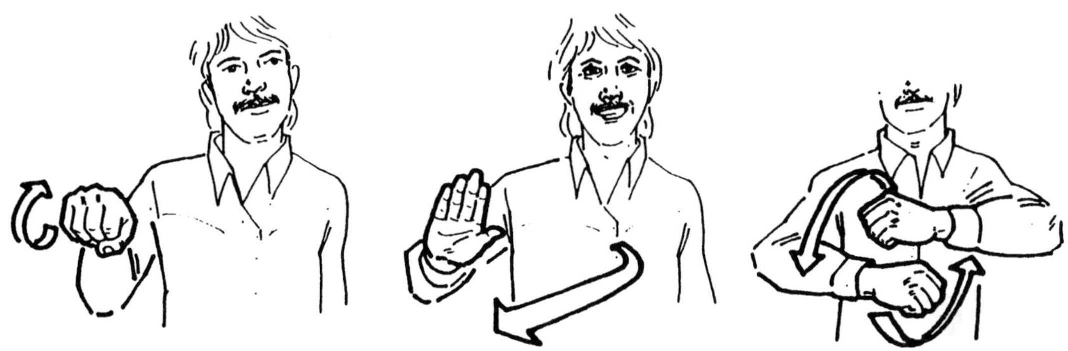

So they all rolled over

And one fell out

(3) There were eight in the bed ...

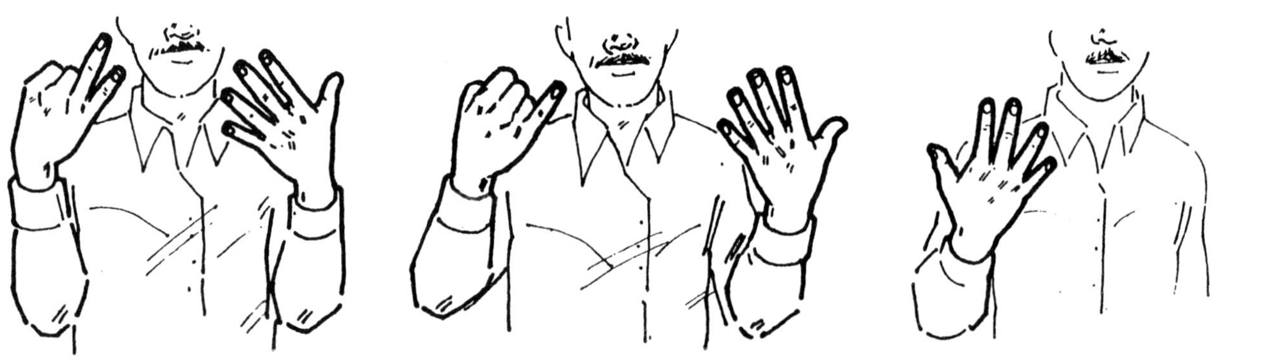

(4) seven in the bed ... **(5)** six in the bed ... **(6)** five in the bed ...

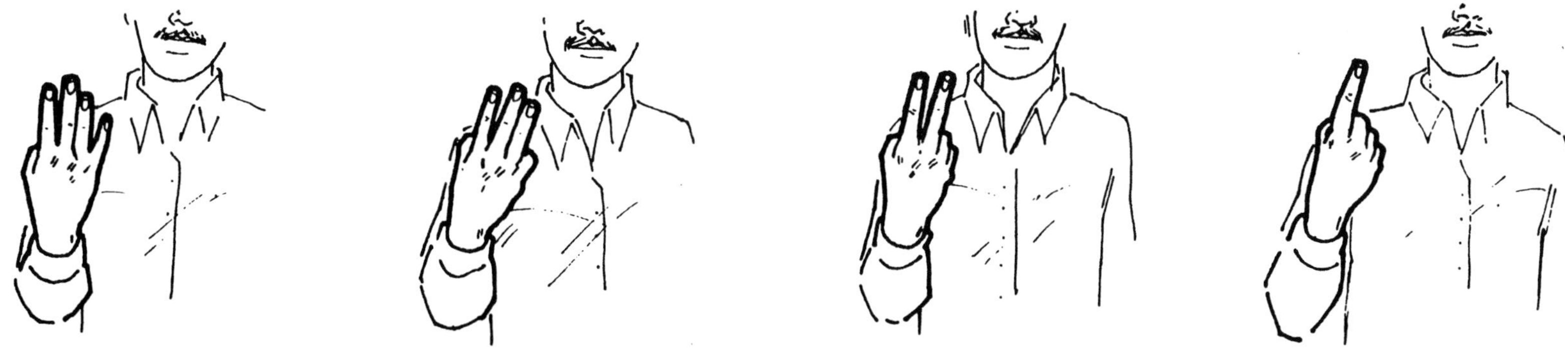

(7) four in the bed ... **(8)** three in the bed ... **(9)** two in the bed ... **(10)** one in the bed ...

(11) There were none in the bed

And the one said "Good night! Good night!"

Old MacDonald

1. Old MacDonald had a farm
E I E I O
And on that farm
He had some cows
E I E I O
With a moo-moo here
And a moo-moo there
Here a moo, there a moo
Everywhere a moo-moo.

2. Old MacDonald had a farm
E I E I O
And on that farm
He had some ducks
E I E I O
With a quack-quack here
And a quack-quack there
Here a quack, there a quack
Everywhere a quack-quack.

3. ... had some sheep
E I E I O
With a baa-baa here
And a baa-baa there ...

4. ... had a cat
E I E I O
With a meow-meow here
And a meow-meow there ...

5. ... had a dog
E I E I O
With a woof-woof here
And a woof-woof there ...

(1) Old MacDonald had a farm

E I E I O

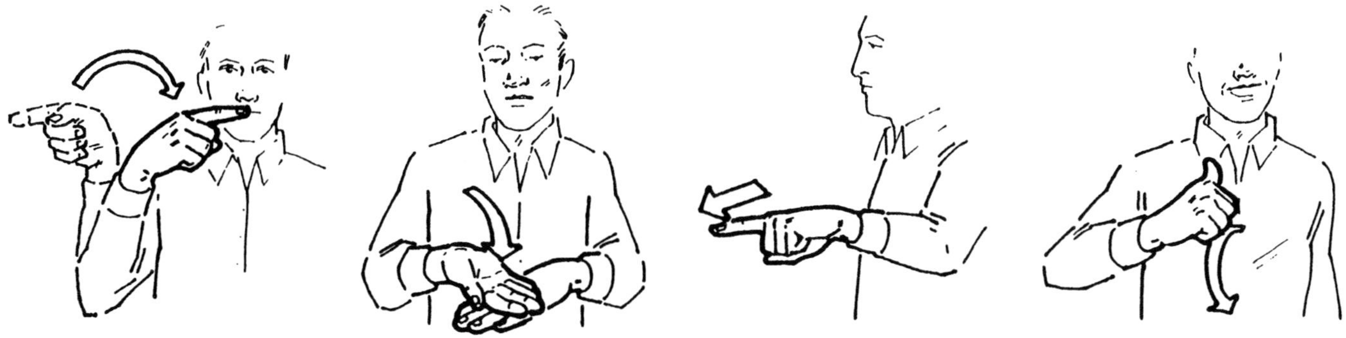

And on that farm

He

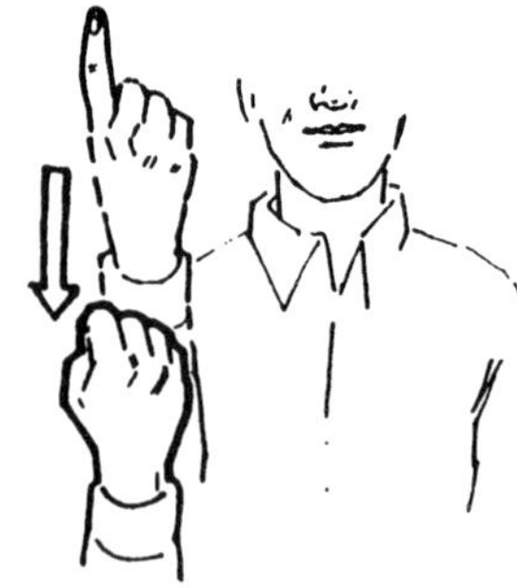
had

some

cows

E

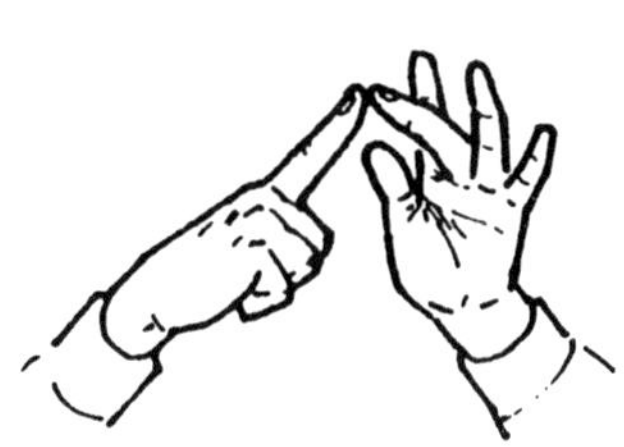
I

E

I

O

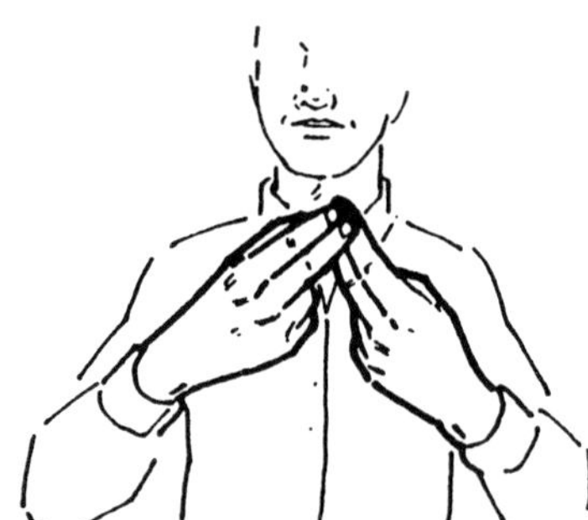
With *a*

moo-moo

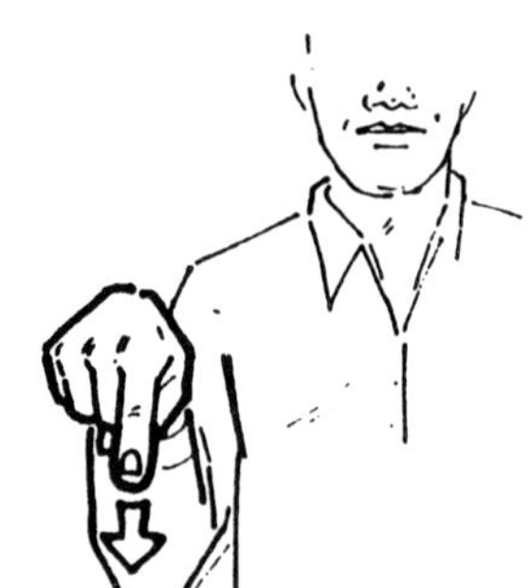
here

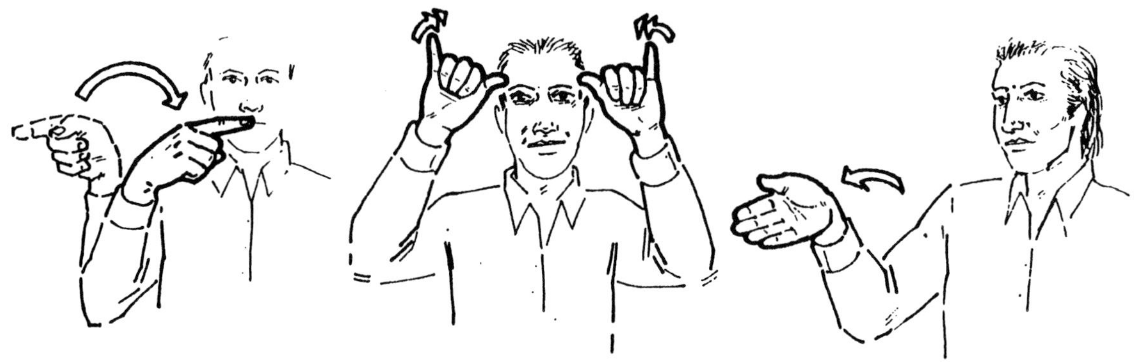

And *a* moo-moo there

Here *a* moo, there *a* moo

Everywhere *a* moo-moo.

(2) Old MacDonald had a farm

E I E I O

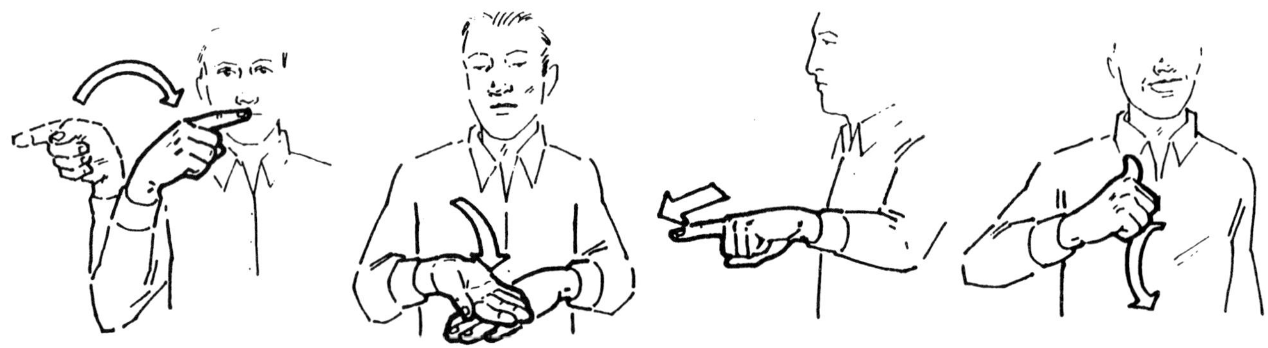

And on that farm

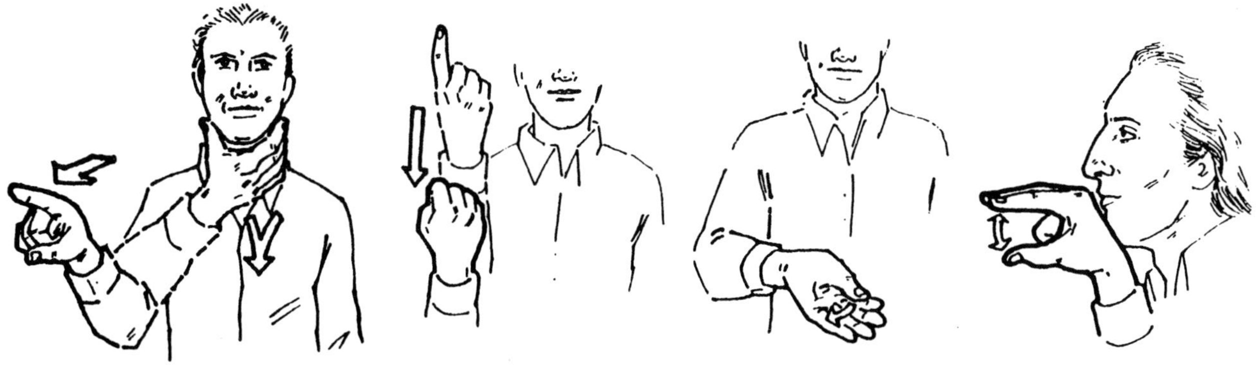

He had some ducks

E I E I O

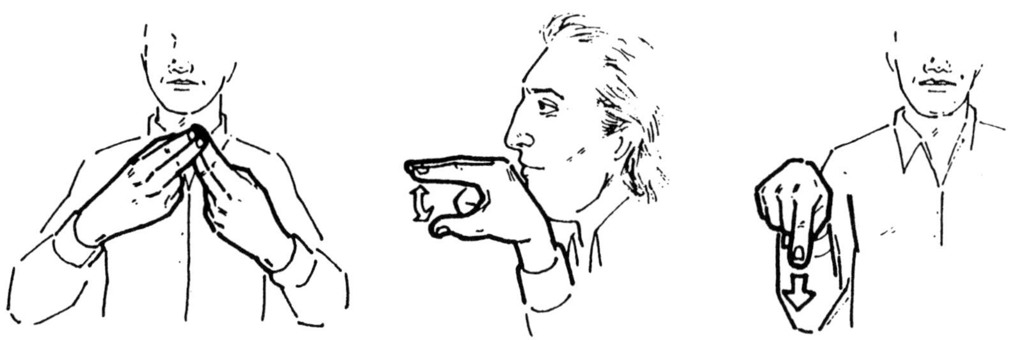

With *a* quack-quack here

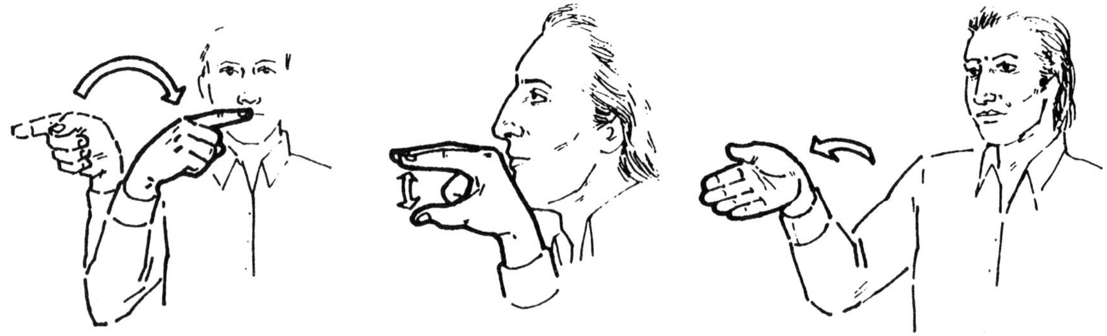

And *a* quack-quack there

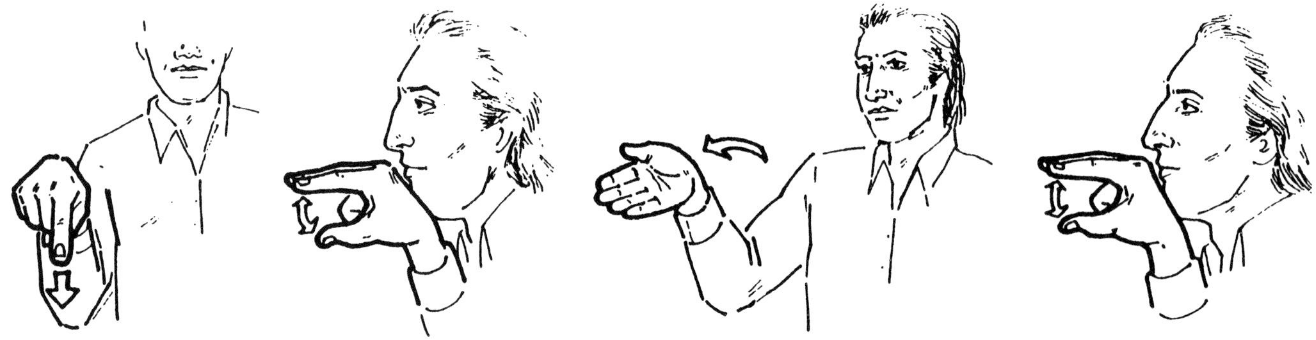

Here *a* quack, there *a* quack

Everywhere *a* quack-quack.

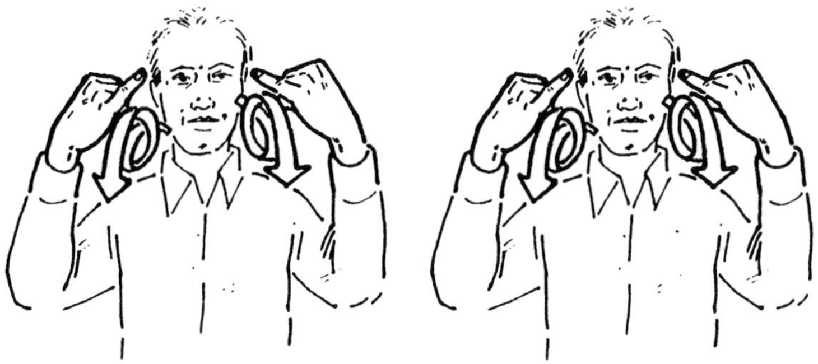

(3) Sheep, baa-baa

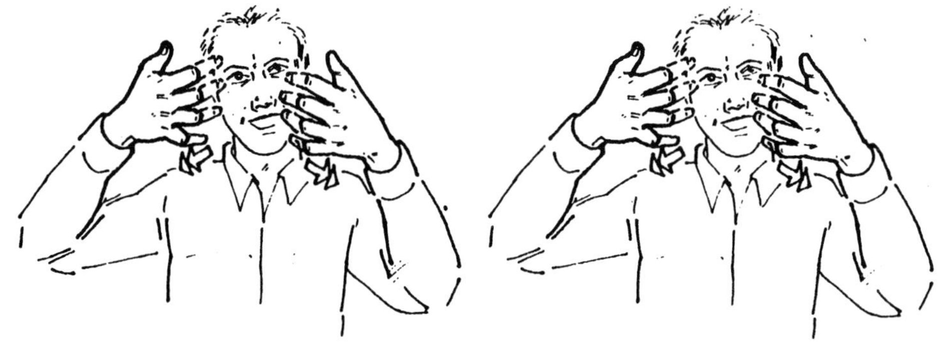

(4) Cat, meow-meow

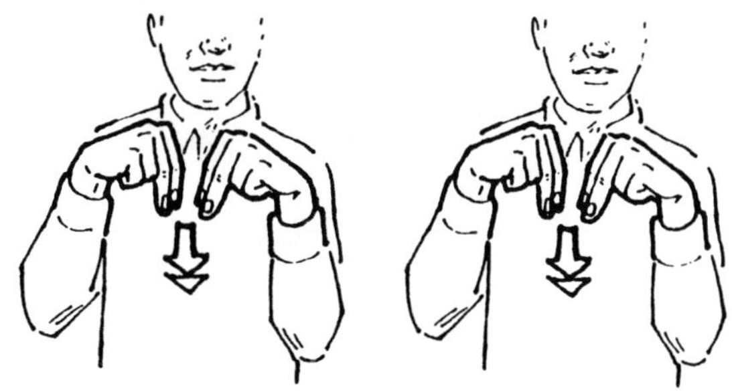

(5) Dog, woof-woof

Stable Song

1. In the stable
Cold and bare
Let us meet
The animals there.

2. Come on donkey let's meet you
Come and say "How do you do?"
Eeaw Eeaw Eeaw Eeaw

3. Come on brown cow let's meet you
Come and say "How do you do?"
Moo-moo Moo-moo Moo-moo Moo-moo

4. Come on woolly-lamb let's meet you
Come and say "How do you do?"
Baa-baa Baa-baa Baa-baa Baa-baa

5. Come on sheep-dog let's meet you
Come and say "How do you do?"
Woof-woof Woof-woof
Woof-woof Woof-woof

6. Come on pink pig let's meet you
Come and say "How do you do?"
Oink-oink Oink-oink
Oink-oink Oink-oink

7. Come on yellow duck let's meet you
Come and say "How do you do?"
Quack-quack Quack-quack
Quack-quack Quack-quack

8. Come on black cat let's meet you
Come and say "How do you do?"
Meow-meow Meow-meow
Meow-meow Meow-meow

(1) In

the

stable

Cold

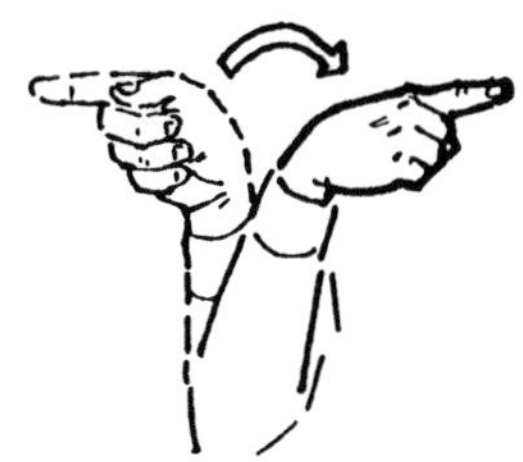

and

bare

Let

us

meet

The animals there.

(2) Come on donkey let's meet you

Come and say "How do you do?"

Eeaw

Eeaw

Eeaw

Eeaw

(3) Come on

brown

cow

let's

meet

you

Come and say "How do you do?"

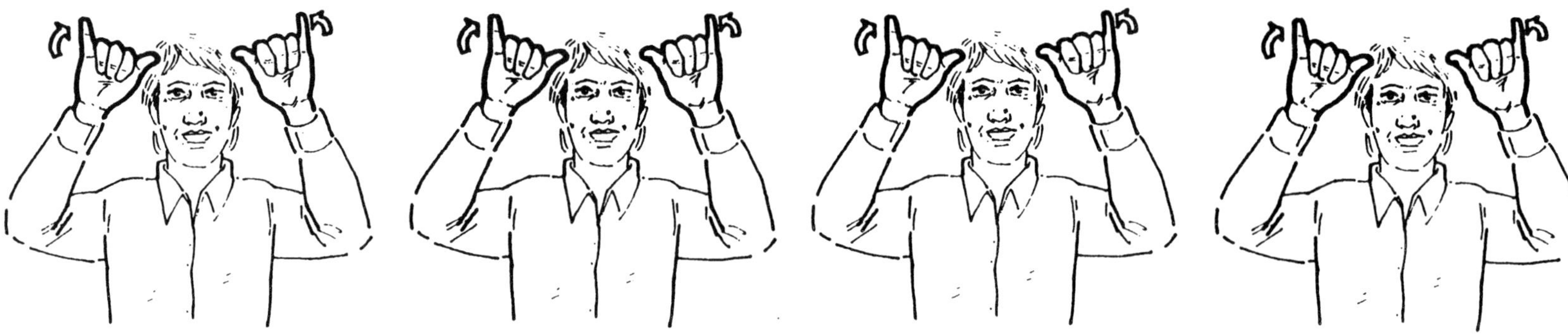

Moo-moo Moo-moo Moo-moo Moo-moo.

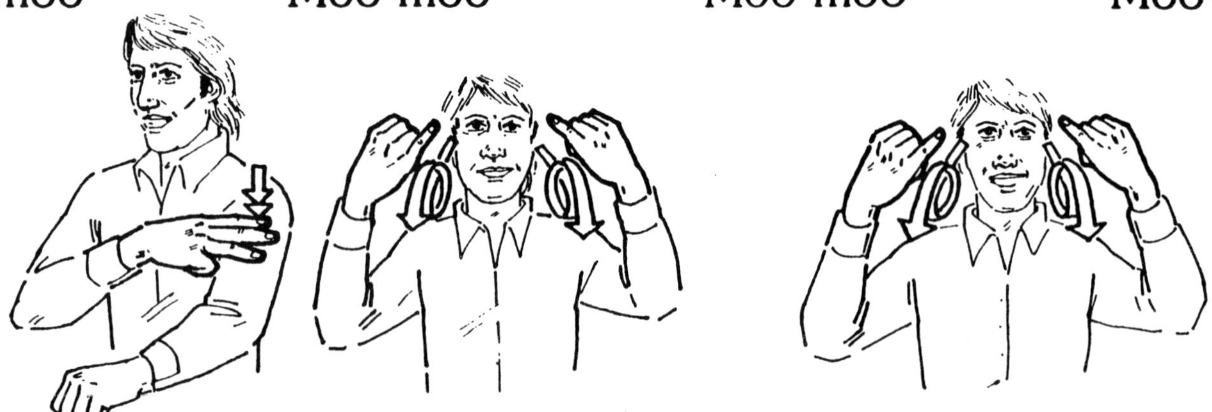

(4) Woolly-lamb, Baa-baa

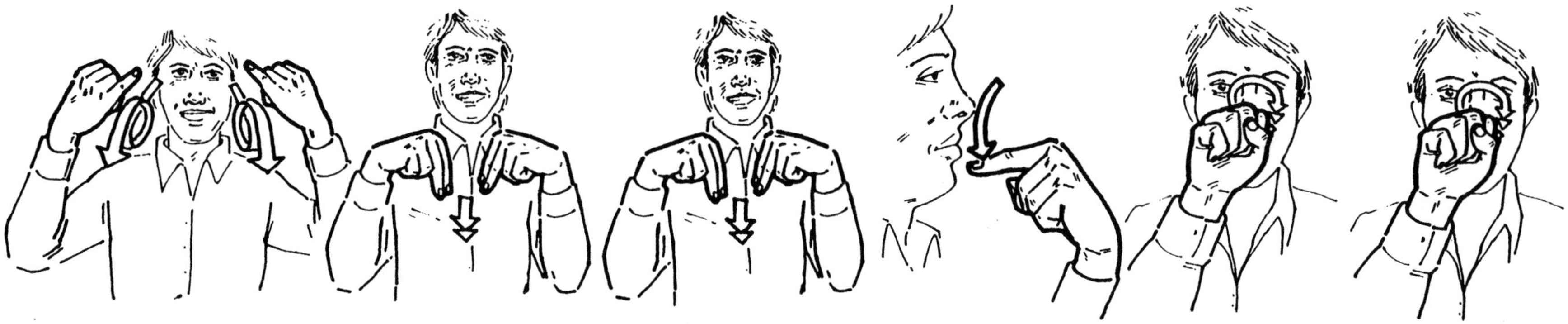

(5) Sheep-dog, Woof-woof (6) Pink pig, Oink-oink

(7) Yellow duck, Quack-quack (8) Black cat, Meow-meow

Wheels on the Bus

1. The wheels on the bus
Go round and round
Round and round
Round and round
The wheels on the bus
Go round and round all day long.

2. The horn on the bus
Goes beep-beep-beep
Beep-beep-beep
Beep-beep-beep
The horn on the bus
Goes beep-beep-beep all day long

3. The wipers on the bus
Go swish-swish-swish
Swish-swish-swish
Swish-swish-swish
The wipers on the bus
Go swish-swish-swish all day long

4. The men on the bus
Go sleep-sleep-sleep
Sleep-sleep-sleep ...

5. The ladies on the bus
Go chatter-chatter-chatter
Chatter-chatter-chatter ...

6. The babies on the bus
Go wah-wah-wah
Wah-wah-wah ...

7. The people on the bus
Go bump-bump-bump
Bump-bump-bump ...

(1) The wheels on the bus

Go round and round, round and round, round and round

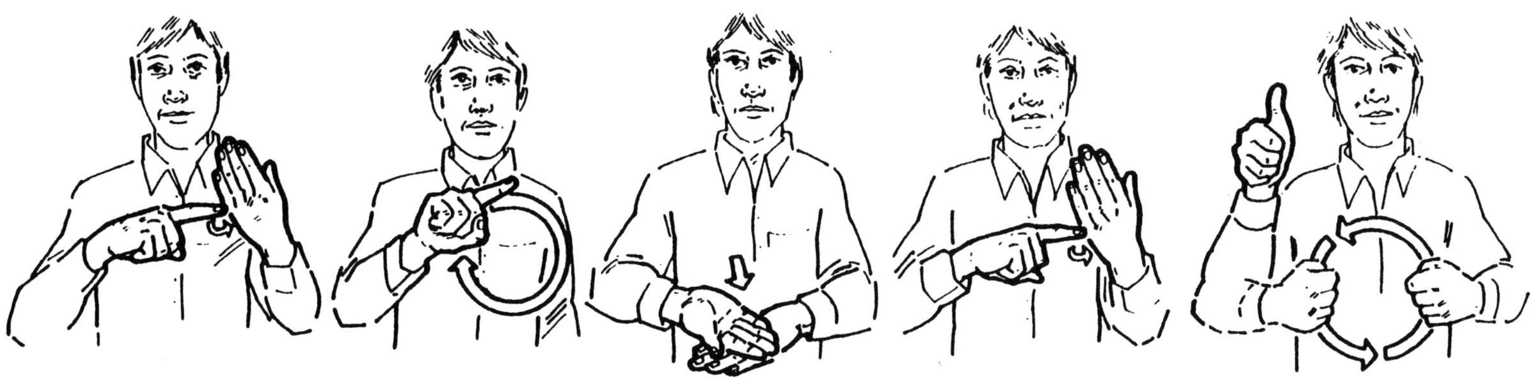

The wheels on the bus

Go round and round all day long.

(2) The horn on the bus

Goes beep-beep-beep, beep-beep-beep, beep-beep-beep

The horn on the bus

Goes beep-beep-beep all day long

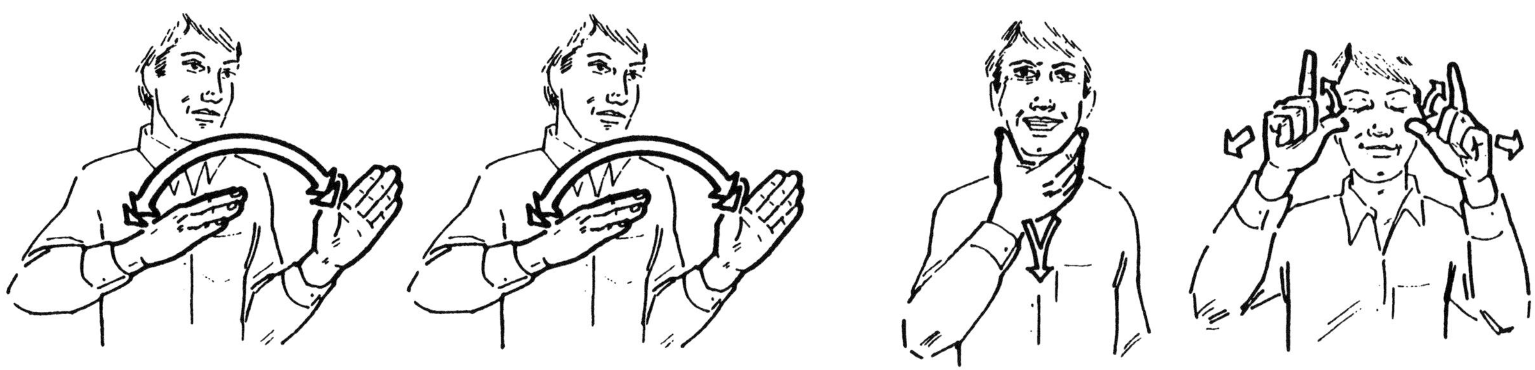

(3) Wipers, swish-swish-swish (4) Men, sleep-sleep-sleep

(5) Ladies, chatter-chatter-chatter

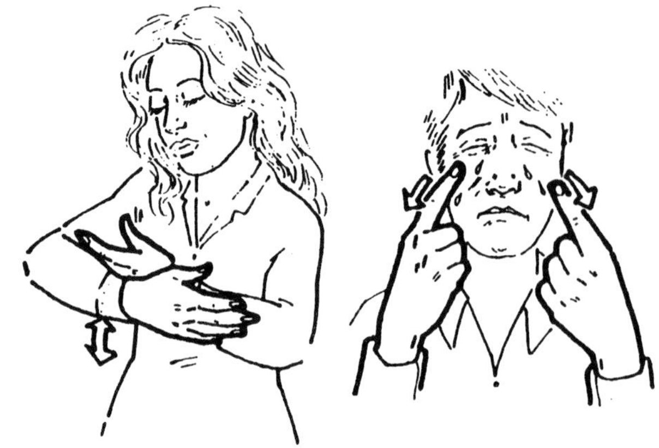

(6) Babies, wah-wah-wah

(7) People, bump-bump-bump

I know an Old Lady

1. I know an old lady
Who swallowed a fly
I don't know why
She swallowed a fly
Perhaps she'll die!

2. I know an old lady
Who swallowed a spider
That wriggled and jiggled and tickled inside her
She swallowed the spider
To catch the fly
I don't know why
She swallowed a fly
Perhaps she'll die!

3. I know an old lady
Who swallowed a bird
How absurd to swallow a bird!
She swallowed the bird
To catch the spider
That wriggled and jiggled and tickled inside her
She swallowed the spider
To catch the fly
I don't know why
She swallowed a fly
Perhaps she'll die!

4. ... swallowed a cat
Fancy that, she swallowed a cat ...

5. ... swallowed a dog
What a hog to swallow a dog ...

6. ... swallowed a goat
She opened her throat
And swallowed a goat ...

7. ... swallowed a cow
I don't know how
She swallowed a cow ...

8. ... swallowed a horse
She's dead of course!

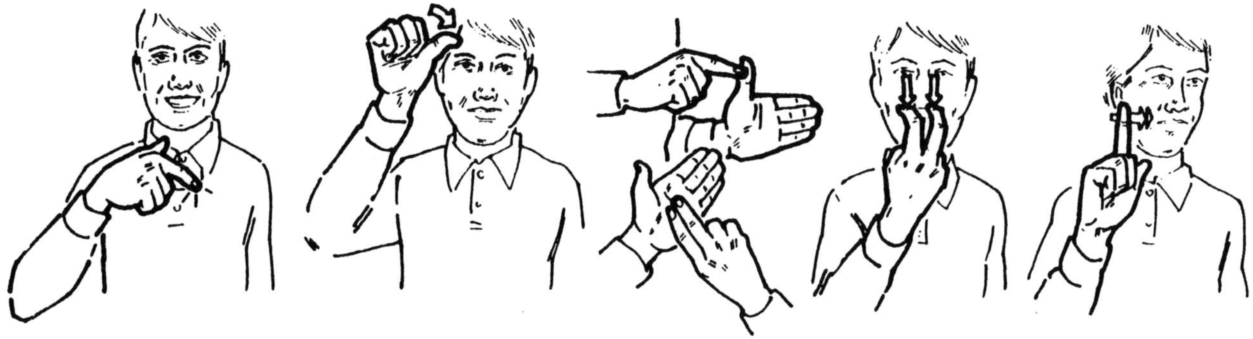

(1) I know an old lady

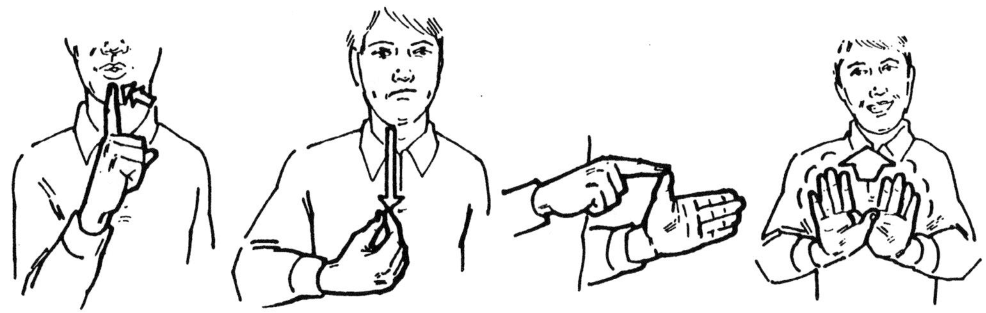

Who swallowed a fly

I don't know why

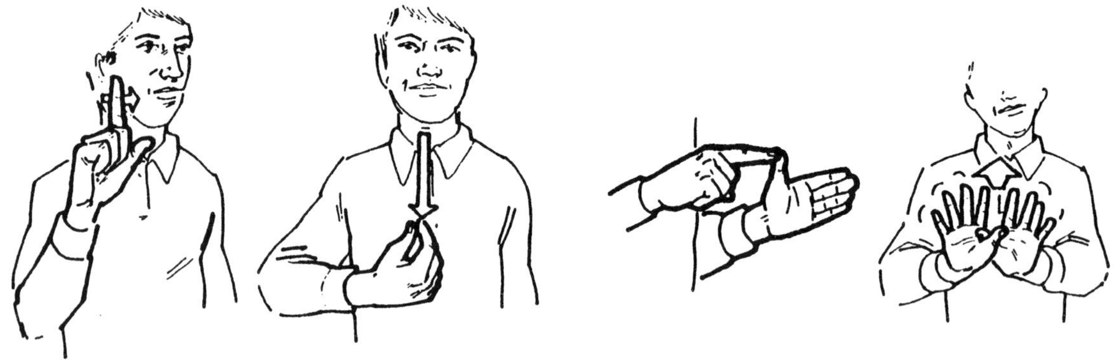

She swallowed a fly

Perhaps she'll die!

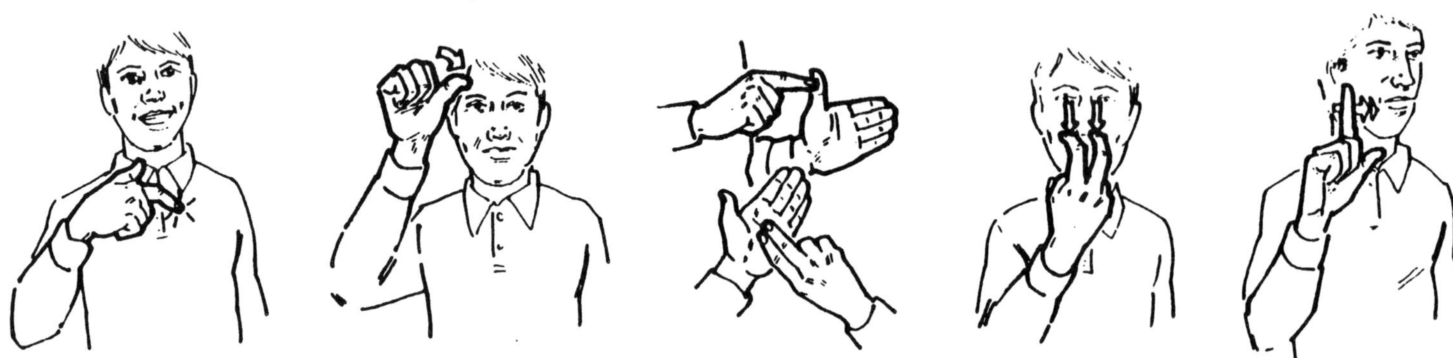

(2) I know an old lady

Who swallowed a spider

That wriggled and jiggled and tickled inside her

She swallowed the spider

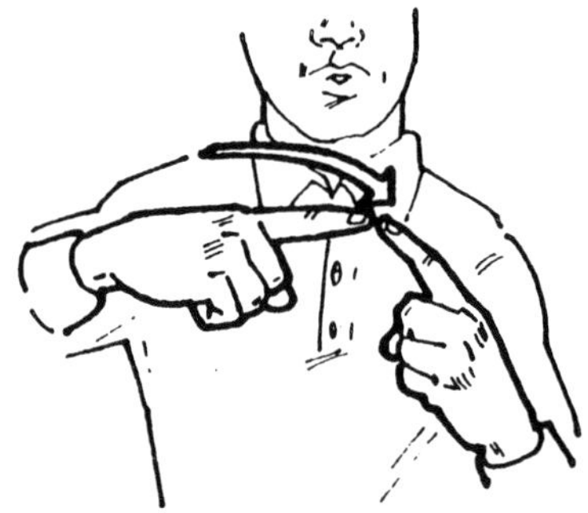

To

catch

the

fly

I

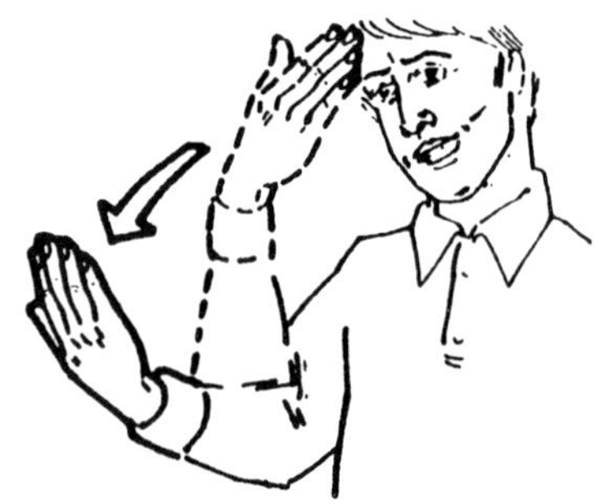

don't know

why

She

swallowed

a

fly

Perhaps

she'll

die!

(3) I

know

an

old

lady

Who

swallowed

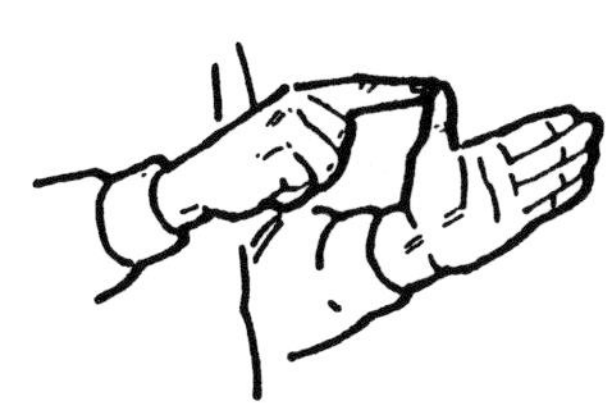
a

bird

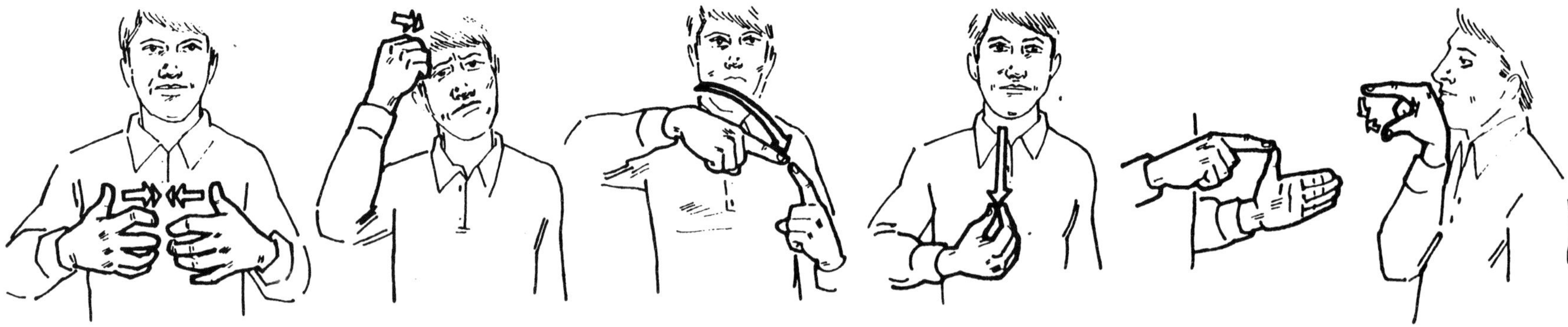

How absurd to swallow a bird!

She swallowed the bird

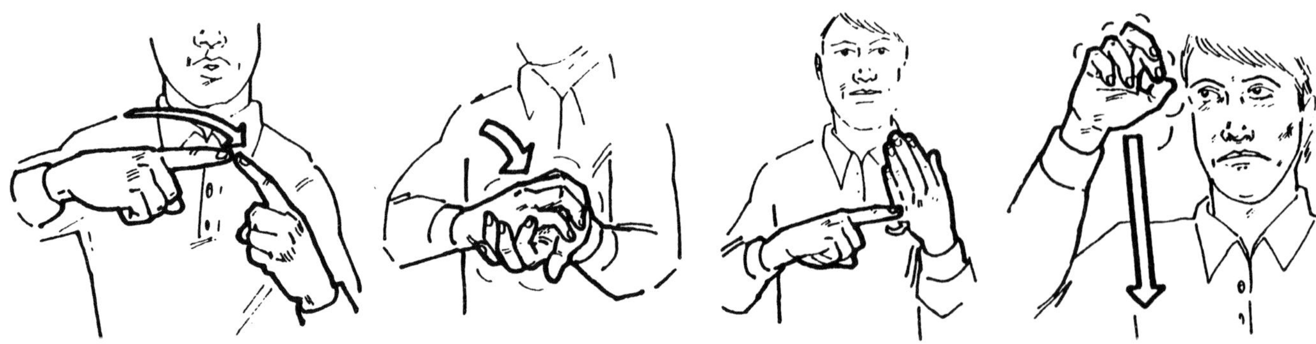

To catch the spider

That wriggled and jiggled and tickled inside her

She swallowed the spider

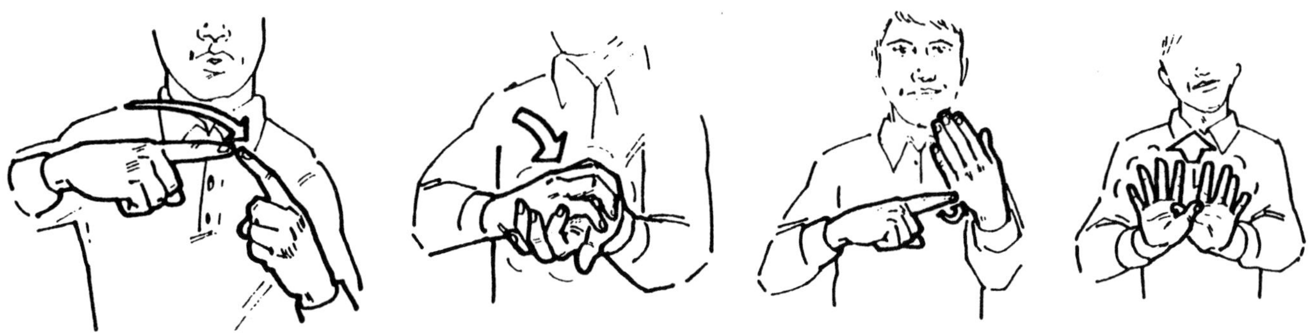

To catch the fly

I

don't know

why

She

swallowed

a

fly

Perhaps

she'll

die!

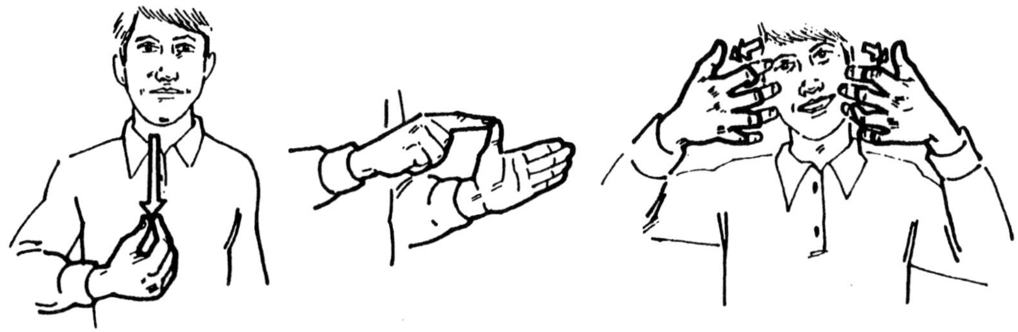

(4) ... swallowed a cat

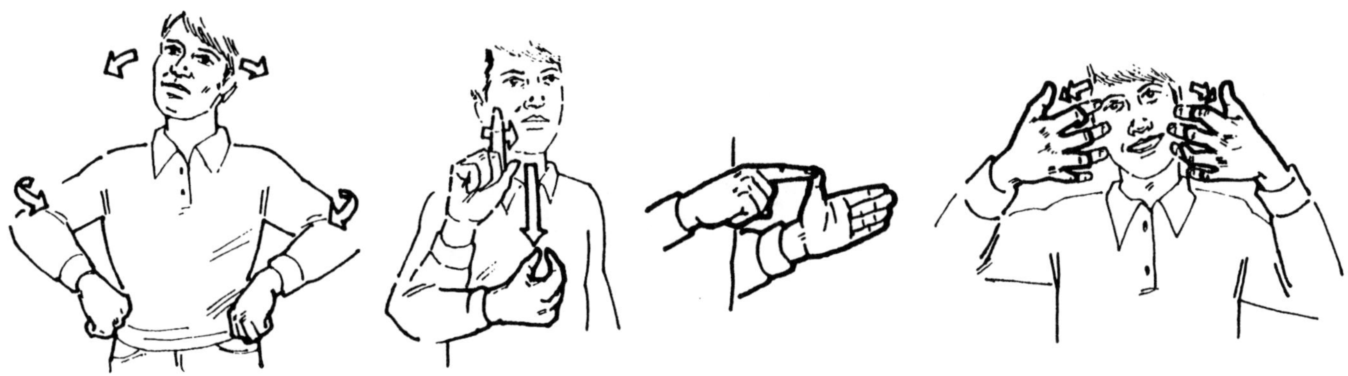

Fancy that, she swallowed a cat.

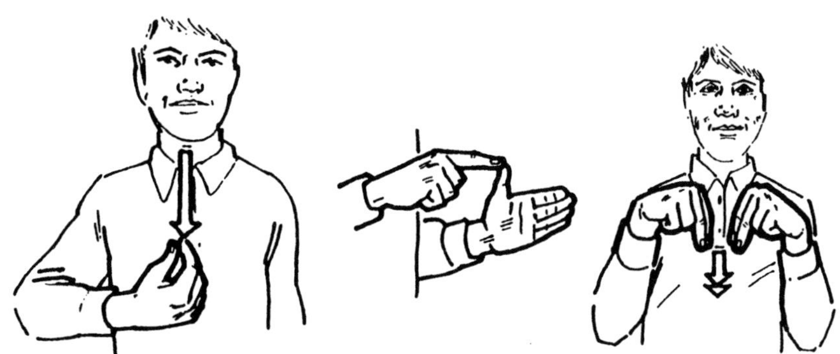

(5) ... swallowed a dog

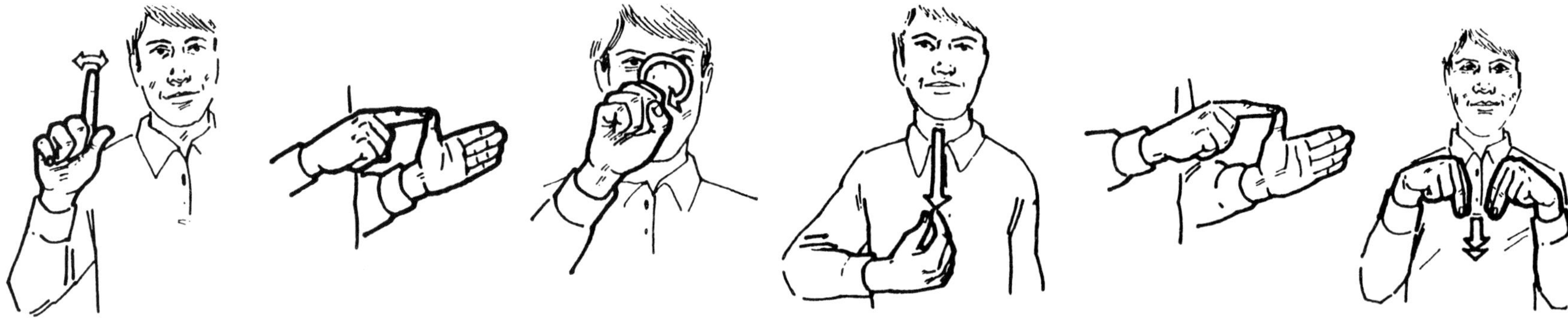

What a hog *to* swallow a dog.

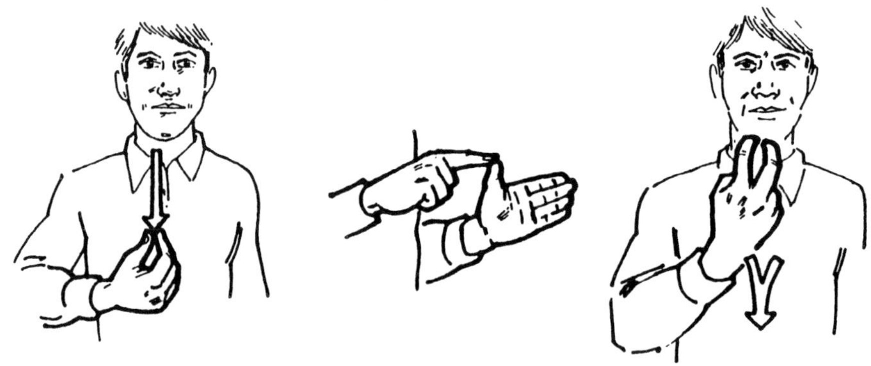

(6) ... swallowed a goat

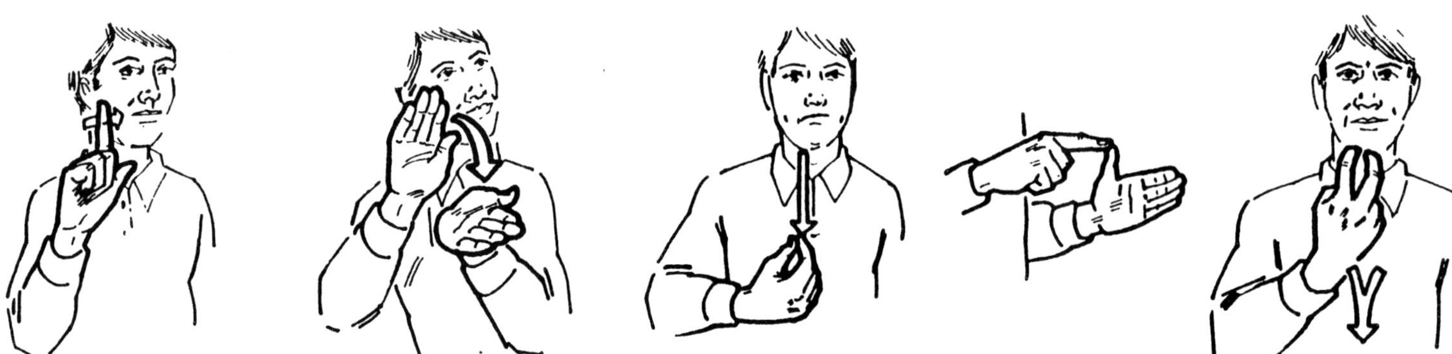

She opened her throat *And* swallowed a goat.

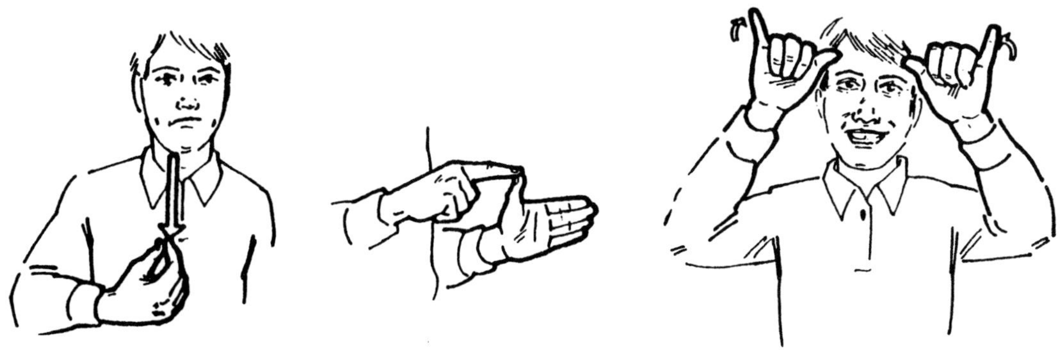

(7) ... swallowed a cow

I don't know how

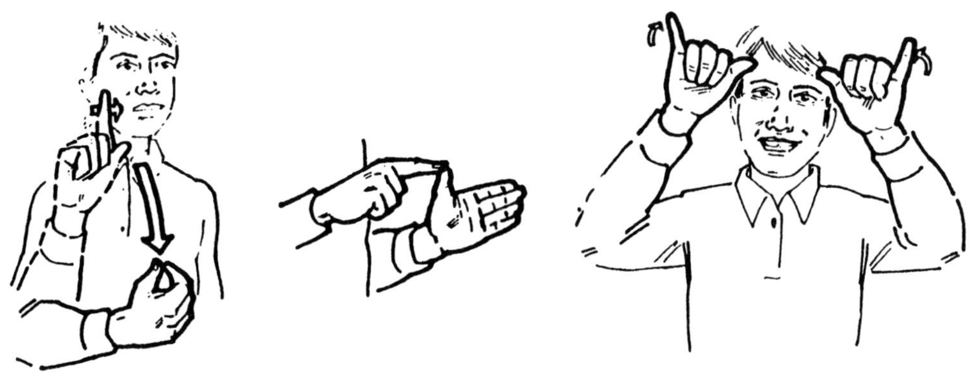

She swallowed a cow.

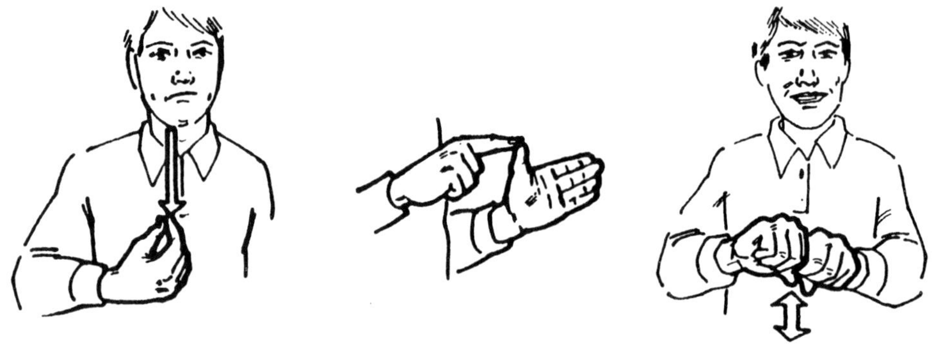

(8) ... swallowed a horse

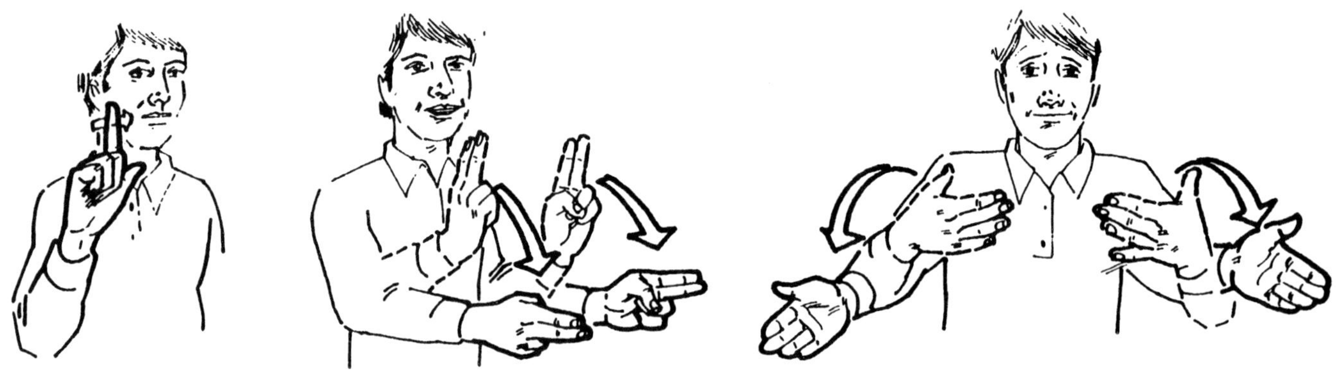

She's dead of course!

Lazy Mary

1. Lazy Mary will you get up!
   Will you get up!
   Will you get up!
   Lazy Mary will you get up!
   Will you get up today!

2. No! No! Mother I won't get up!
   I won't get up!
   I won't get up!
   No! No! Mother I won't get up!
   I won't get up today!

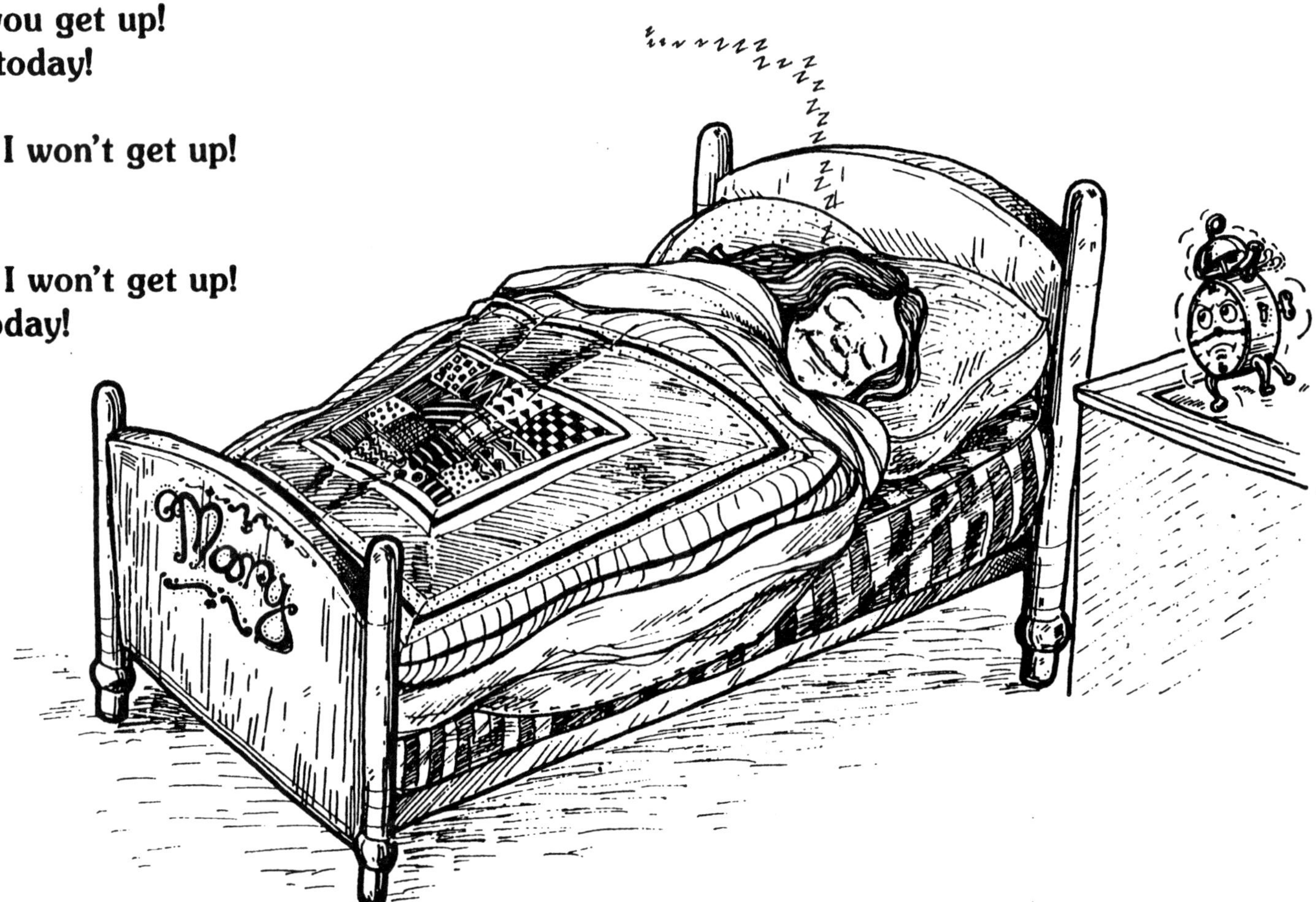

(1) Lazy

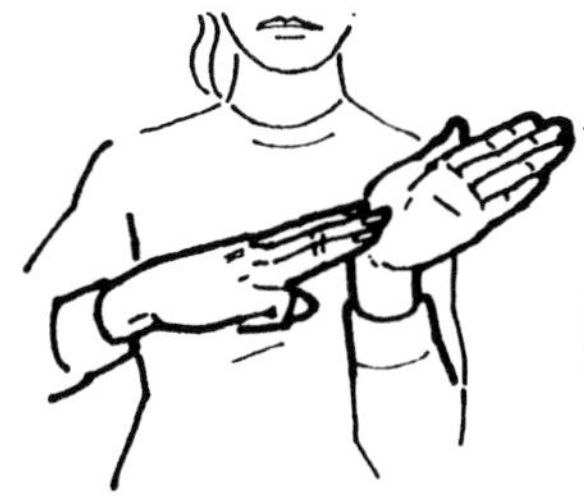

Mary

will you

get up!

Will you

get up!

Will you

get up!

Lazy

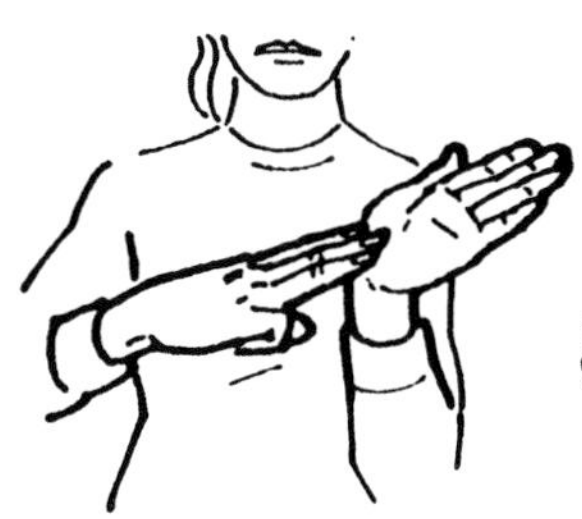

Mary

will you

get up!

Will you get up today!

(2) No! No! Mother I won't get up!

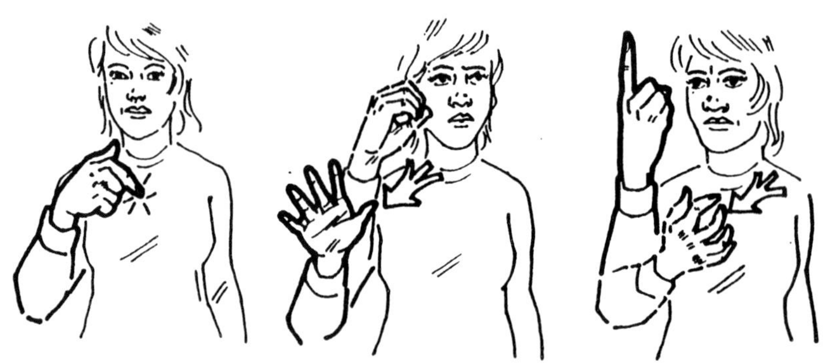

I won't get up!

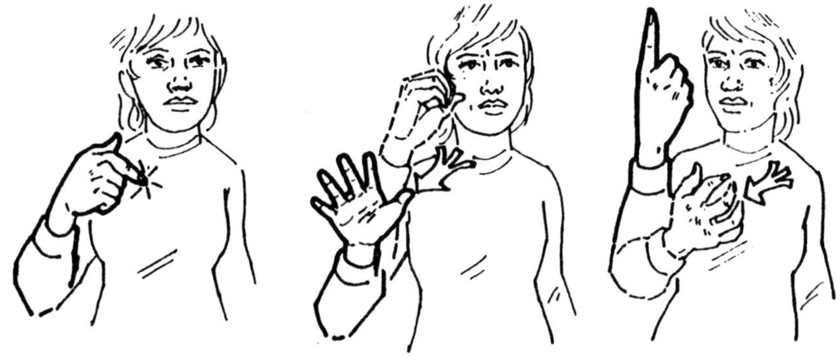

I won't get up!

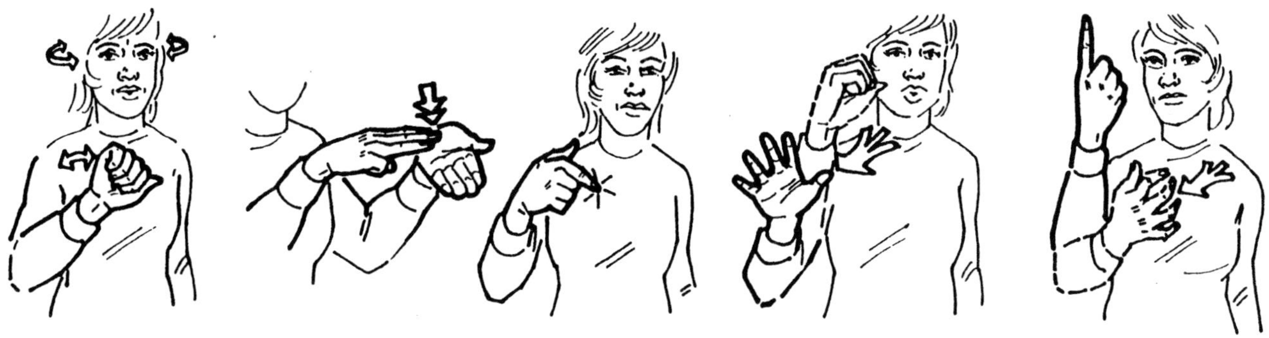

No! No! Mother I won't get up!

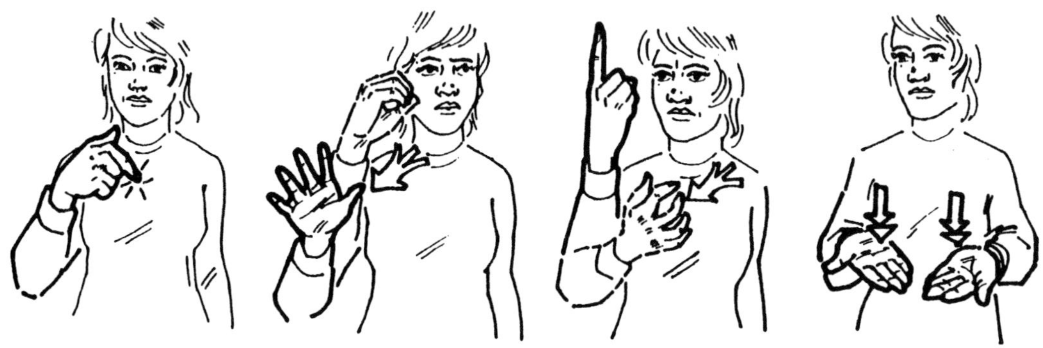

I won't get up today!